ARCHITECTURE AS PEACEWORK

RUDOLF STEINER (1915)

ARCHITECTURE AS PEACEWORK

The First Goetheanum, Dornach, 1914

Five Lectures given in Dornach, Switzerland
October 10–25, 1914

TRANSLATION AND COMMENTARY BY FREDERICK AMRINE

INTRODUCTION BY JOHN KETTLE

RUDOLF STEINER

SteinerBooks

CW 287

SteinerBooks
Anthropposophic Press

610 Main Street
Great Barrington, Massachusetts 01230
www.steinerbooks.org

Original translation from the German by Frederick Amrine.

This book is volume 287 in the Collected Works (CW) of Rudolf Steiner, published by SteinerBooks, 2017. The translation is based on the second German edition of GA 287, *Der Dornacher Bau als Wahrzeichen geschichtlichen Werdens und künstlerischer Umwandlungsimpulse*, published by Rudolf Steiner Verlag, Dornach, Switzerland, 1985.

Print: 978-1-62148-099-0
e-Book: 978-1-62148-100-3

Printed in the United States of America

CONTENTS

The publishers wish to thank the Provost's Office; the College of Literature, Science, and the Arts; and the Department of Germanic Languages and Literatures at the University of Michigan for providing a generous subsidy for the publication of this volume.

On the publication of Rudolf Steiner's lectures

The written works of Rudolf Steiner are the foundation of anthroposophical spiritual science. In addition to the books he wrote, Steiner also offered numerous lectures and courses, both public and private, between 1900 and 1924, intended specifically for members of the Theosophical (later Anthroposophical) Society. Initially he did not want his lectures to be set down in writing, since they were intended as "verbal communications not meant for print." But after an increasing number of incomplete and erroneous transcripts of these lectures were printed and distributed by attendees, it became clear that he needed to regulate the publication process. He entrusted this task to Marie Steiner-von Sivers. It was incumbent upon her to arrange for the stenographers and to oversee the entire process. Since there was never enough time for Rudolf Steiner to correct the transcripts himself, except in a very few instances, his disclaimer must be taken into consideration in regard to all of his published lectures: "It must simply be accepted that errors are to be found in the drafts, which I have not looked through myself." After the death of Marie Steiner in 1948, work on a collected edition of all of Rudolf Steiner's writings and lectures began, in keeping with her guidelines. This volume is part of that edition.

INTRODUCTION

The main theme of this book is the architecture of the Goetheanum, the exquisite, startlingly original new building that was under construction at the time, and in the place, at which Rudolf Steiner gave these five lectures—the month of October 1914 in Dornach, Switzerland. Construction had reached the stage of topping off six months earlier; that is, the main structural elements were in place and the roof was covered. Steiner concentrates on the significance of the building's columns and domes, how they are to be looked at, how their spiritual inventiveness is to be read, and how he expects they will be received by anthroposophists and others. He knows that the building is one more challenge to convention, filled with complexities that will probably be difficult for many to understand: "a new style of building that is connected to the mysteries of the cosmos."[1] In his final lecture in the series, excited by thoughts of the building's leap into the future, he says, "It will be apparent to you from many things that have been said here recently that the art in our building must contain a new element that has not hitherto existed in the evolution of art, but is essential for the further progress of humanity."

As we read—as we would have heard had we been in that audience—we find Steiner searching for an image that will convey the magical quality of the paintings that will fill the building's two overlapping domes. He pictures Greek, Roman, Renaissance, even nineteenth-century painting, as a statue, its gesture unmoving: "That's how we might describe the evolution of the arts that we can follow up to our own epoch. We can look upon it as something that is standing in a resting pose, and our intention is to speak the magic word that will make it walk, bring it to life inwardly, bring it into movement."

1 For a fuller description of the building, complete with over a hundred photographs, see Rudolf Steiner, *The First Goetheanum: Toward a New Theory of Architecture*, CW 290, forthcoming from SteinerBooks.

Clearly, for him the Goetheanum rising out of the hilltop is much more than a place to stage plays or hold meetings. It will embody the sum of what he has learned, what he has taught: "Everything we have absorbed of spiritual science in the course of the years, and a great deal more besides, is expressed in this building."

When he speaks of the arts in the building, he is most eloquent on painting, looking for a way to describe his new approach. Though what was still most common in the arts at that time was the realistic representation of people, places, and things, there had been astounding eruptions of non-representational painting in the first dozen years of the century. In 1911, for instance, Wassily Kandinsky, an earnest student of anthroposophy, and Franz Marc announced the first exhibition of their new group of artists *Der Blaue Reiter* (The Blue Rider) in these words:

> *The great upheaval,*
> *The shifting emphasis in art, literature, and music,*
> *The multifariousness of form, the constructive principle, the composition of these forms*
> *The intensive turn to the inner realm of nature and, associated with it, the rejection of the beautification of nature's exterior*
> *—Such are, generally sketched out, the signs of the new inner renaissance.*[2]

Around Europe were painters like Picasso, Klee, Léger, Modigliani, Mondrian, all involved to some extent in this great upheaval. This was the revolutionary background against which Steiner was finding his own ways to represent the physical world and the spiritual world together. For him, all was new. The artist, he insisted, must liberate color from what is perceived in nature or in life, must not hesitate to change one color for another. The painter must perceive and experience colors arising "through their own inherent impulse—things will not be as they are in nature, but rather as they are in the spiritual world."

---

[2] Tracey Bashkoff and Megan M. Fontanella, organizers, *The Great Upheaval: Modern Art from the Guggenheim Collection, 1910-1918* (New York: Guggenheim Museum Publications, 2011), p. 15.

As usual in his lecture series, Steiner has much to say on other topics: the worldwide growth of materialism; the time in the future when not just physical evolution but spiritual evolution will reach its end; the way historical documents conceal the truth of what happened in the past; even the distant prospect that humanity will eventually be resurrected in other planets.

And there are at least half a dozen direct references to World War I in the five lectures. One can continually feel how much Steiner was distracted by this huge conflict that was gradually spreading throughout Europe and shattering its peace. The lectures were given on three weekends in October 1914, ten to twelve weeks after war broke out. For Steiner, even the horrors of the battlefield were outweighed by what happened in the spiritual world. "Never before have I myself seen anything as astounding as what followed upon the assassination at Sarajevo. . . . In the spiritual world exactly the opposite effect was produced than had been produced in the physical world. In the physical world, fear held back the war; in the spiritual world it was an element that hastened on the war."

The aggressively militant, assertive stance and language of German politicians and newspapers stimulated Steiner to seek peaceful, balanced, reasonable ways of speaking about the war, the apportioning of blame, the description of aims, and the final outcome. He found the press particularly irresponsible, even more than those in government and the armed forces. Steiner was also dismayed by the way the government was pressing the German population to support the uncritical nationalism of its propaganda, and said so: in lecture three of this book, for example, Steiner asserts that "The individual human being stands higher than the nation!" This was an act that required some courage, since though resident in Switzerland he continued to lecture in Germany throughout the war, giving well over two hundred lectures there, half of them in the country's capital of Berlin.

The theme of peace is a notable feature of the lectures, a powerful counterpoint to the disaster that had started in a part of the continent he knew well and that was now spreading until it surrounded the peaceful country of Switzerland. The incident in June 1914 that had pulled much of Europe into war in the space of five weeks was the murder of Archduke Franz Ferdinand of Austria-Hungary and his wife Sophie in Sarajevo, the capital of Austria-Hungary's recently acquired province of Bosnia. They were shot by an assassin of the Black Hand, a revolutionary organization formed by a group that included the intelligence chief of the Serbian army. Their aim was to achieve "the unification of all Serbs," by violent means if necessary.[3]

Steiner was the son of an Austrian whose work for the Austrian Southern Railway gave him employment around the Austro-Hungarian empire, which at its height incorporated Austria, Hungary, parts of northeast Italy, Slovenia, the Czech Republic, Slovakia, Croatia-Slavonia, Bosnia & Herzegovina, the northern part of Serbia-Montenegro, Romania, the southwest of Ukraine, west Moldova, and a fragment of Bulgaria. Steiner was born in Kraljevec and raised until age eight there and in other villages in the Kingdom of Croatia-Slavonia, a nominally autonomous, ethnically Croatian and Serbian kingdom within the empire. When he was eight, his father's promotion to stationmaster took the family to Neudörfl in Hungary, where as a German-speaking Austrian he was again regarded as a foreigner, this time by his Hungarian-speaking school fellows. Treated as an outsider, he knew at first-hand the resentment that citizens who didn't speak German felt for the co-governing Austrians. As Stewart Easton put it in his biography of Steiner, he "as a boy experienced in his own person not only the division between east and west, but more particularly the clash of cultures in the Austro-Hungarian Empire"[4] —resentment that was most deeply felt by the Slavs inside and outside the boundaries of the empire and that eventually led to the assassination of the archduke.[5]

---

3 John Simkin, *First World War Encyclopedia* (Spartacus Educational, 2012).

4 Stewart C. Easton, *Rudolf Steiner: Herald of a New Epoch* (Hudson, NY: Anthroposophic Press, 1980), p. 14.

5 Christopher Clark, *The Sleepwalkers: How Europe Went to War in 1914* (New York: HarperCollins, 2012), p. xxviii. Clark added: "The fact that Serbian-dominated Yugoslavia emerged as one of the victor states of the war seemed implicitly to vindicate the act of the man who pulled the trigger on 28 June. Certainly that was the view of the Yugoslav authorities, who marked the spot where he did so with bronze footprints and a plaque celebrating the assassin's 'first steps into Yugoslav freedom'."

Speaking in 1916, Steiner said "... the death of the Archduke Ferdinand of Austria is one of those concealed events of the present day, despite all that occurred on the external physical plane.... What rose up as the soul of Franz Ferdinand into the spiritual worlds became a focal point for very strong, powerful forces, and much of what is now happening is connected with the very fact that a unique transition took place between life and so-called death, so that this soul became something quite different from what other souls become."... "You might indeed call him an intense friend of all that belongs to the Slavs. He understood—or perhaps I should say: something living in him of which he was not fully aware understood—what forms would be necessary for the social life of the Slavs if they were to develop as individual peoples."[6] But "in removing Franz Ferdinand from the scene, the Serbian terrorists ensured that there would be no voice of moderation in Vienna," a historian has written.[7]

The first lecture in this book, given on October 10, came ten weeks after the start of the war, when the German army moved into Luxembourg on its way to Belgium and France. In those ten weeks the German and French armies had fought a number of intensive battles, and the Germans had just failed to capture Paris. Casualties on both sides had been huge.

The vast scale and violence of the war astonished the continent. Few adults had any experience of a large-scale war. The last great war, the Franco-Prussian war of 1870-71, was two generations in the past. It had lasted ten months and the casualties (killed or wounded) had numbered about a quarter of a million. The first great battle of the 1914 war, the Marne, had caused half a million casualties in a week. By November, a month after the last lecture in this book was given, nearly two million men had died in the German, French, and British armies.[8]

---

6 Steiner, *The Karma of Untruthfulness: Secret Societies, the Media, and Preparations for the Great War*, volume 1, lecture 3, Dornach, December 10, 1916. (Rudolf Steiner Press, 2005), p. 56; p. 63.

7 Margaret MacMillan, *The War that Ended Peace: The Road to 1914* (New York: Random House, 2013).

8 http://www.firstworldwar.com/battles/marne1.htm

The war shocked and disoriented people all over the continent. Gradually all the major powers were drawn in: not just Germany, France, and Britain, but also Austria-Hungary and Russia. Belgium was involved from the very start of the war; the British involvement soon brought in Australia and Canada. The Ottoman Empire and Italy, the United States, even small countries such as Siam, Panama, and San Marino were caught up in the war. Altogether forty countries were fighting in what truly was the first world war.

In Switzerland, which was not in the war, Steiner's Goetheanum had been under construction for almost a year, using a large group of volunteers from many countries to work on the building. When war broke out, the anthroposophists among them decided "we must commit ourselves more emphatically to our common cause," according to the account given by one of the volunteers, the Russian symbolist poet Andrei Belyi; "all of us—Russians, Germans, Austrians, French, Poles—we are all brothers in misfortune, we are all victims of criminal politics." But in October nationalism broke out among the workers. "The first momentum of our spontaneous solidarity was quite evidently broken. . . . [T]he storms in the canteen did not abate. . . . Soon, theoretical debates changed to concrete incidents and endangered the whole life of Dornach." Steiner intervened, not blaming any country for the war but instead giving five lectures "concerning the essence of culture. . . . Everyone was enthused. The doctor had succeeded in smoothing the waves of nationalistic passion. . . . [F]rom then on, the members of the various nations at war with one another lived in peace."[9] The "five lectures" Belyi refers to are the lectures in this book. At their heart stands Steiner's resonant exhortation to create "an energetic culture of peace."[10]

After the war it was asserted that Steiner had influenced some decisions of the German army staff in the early months of the war. What had happened was something more personal. Eliza von Moltke, a theosophist and later founding member of the Anthroposophical Society living in Berlin, knew Steiner and invited him to her house.

---

[9] Andrei Belyi, Assya Turgenieff, and Margarita Voloschin, *Reminiscences of Rudolf Steiner* (Ghent, NY: Adonis Press, 1987), pp. 53-56.

[10] See the end of Lecture Two.

She was the wife of Helmuth von Moltke, a high-ranking officer in the German army; through her, von Moltke learned about anthroposophy and found what he called Steiner's "philosophizing" more comprehensible than anyone else's.[11] In 1906 von Moltke was promoted to chief of the German general staff, that is, wartime leader of the army, a post he knew he was unsuited for but which he apparently accepted principally because of his friendship with Kaiser Wilhelm II.[12]

For a decade the army had had a plan devised by von Moltke's predecessor Schlieffen for a European war that involved encircling Paris. In July, probably, "[a]t a time when war seemed imminent but was not yet certain," Stewart Easton wrote, von Moltke "had asked Steiner to pay him a visit as soon as he could, as he was anxious for an intimate talk with him. . . . As it turned out, no meeting between the two men could be arranged before August 27, by which time the German offensive was already more than three weeks old. During this period von Moltke had been compelled to make numerous decisions on the basis of insufficient information, and some of them were obviously faulty." The Schlieffen plan when enacted fell short. "The military decisions made by von Moltke on August 27 and then eight days later, when the decisive mistake was made, did lead to the failure of the great offensive and ultimately to the loss of the war." Von Moltke was forced to resign. After the war Steiner told a reporter that he and von Moltke had discussed only personal matters. Even so, Easton wrote, "Steiner was blamed by nationalistic Germans for the defeat of the battle of the Marne, and he was accused of having used his 'magical powers' on General von Moltke."[13]

As the war began to wind down, Steiner shared his hopes of finding

---

[11] T. H. Meyer (ed.), *Light for the New Millennium: Rudolf Steiner's Association with Helmuth and Eliza von Moltke, Letters, Documents, and After-Death Communications* (London: Temple Lodge, 1997).

[12] "Moltke . . . characterized himself to Prince von Bülow: 'I do not lack personal courage, but I lack the power of rapid decision; I am too reflective, too scrupulous, or, if you like, too conscientious for such a post. I lack the capacity for risking all on a single throw.'" Max Hastings, *Catastrophe: Europe Goes to War* (William Collins, 2013), p. 28.

[13] Easton, pp. 219-223.

how the lives of different peoples and countries could be arranged so that their relations would not lead to future wars. He had discussed these concerns with, among others, a member of the Bavarian state council, Count Otto Lerchenfeld, an anthroposophist who was also concerned about the deep divisions among Europeans. In 1917, as the stalemate on the battle fronts continued and peace remained elusive, Lerchenfeld asked Steiner if he had any idea how a lasting peace could be established. "For three weeks, day after day, he and Steiner worked together over the ideas he had outlined until the entire organic structure for a new social order had been built up," Stewart Easton wrote.[14] The response Steiner gave was the outline of what later became the Threefold Social Order.

In July of that year Steiner considered how he could influence the Austrian government to start preparing for peace negotiations. He knew members of the government and submitted a memorandum that included this sentence: "When human beings become free, so will the nations become free through them." The effort was not fruitful, however.[15]

The principal concern of these five lectures is the first Goetheanum building, that remarkable, innovative structure, first used in the fall of 1920 and still not completely finished when it was destroyed by fire on New Year's Eve, 1922. They were given at the start of a murderous war that directly affected Steiner's life in Dornach and in Germany. The lectures demand to be read because of the insight they give into Steiner's understanding and creativity in the arts, but the fact that throughout those war years he was seeking for peaceful ways for people and countries to live together gives them an added and special significance.

---

[14] Easton, pp. 230-232.

[15] Terry Boardman, Afterword to Rudolf Steiner, *Towards Social Renewal: Rethinking the Basis of Society* (London: Rudolf Steiner Press, 1999), p. 123.

ARCHITECTURE AS PEACEWORK

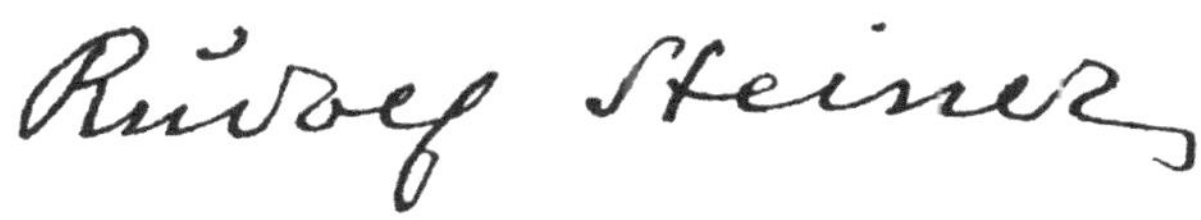

1. *Rudolf Steiner at the building site*

2. *First Goetheanum, from the south*

3. *First Goetheanum, under construction in February 1914*

4. *Detail of the interior construction of the large dome, June 1914*

Lecture 1

Dornach, October 10, 1914

In my lectures I have often described a scenario that could very well have happened in real life, by way of showing how important it is to look beyond superficial appearances, and not to be satisfied by the first impression, as it were. The scenario is as follows. A man is walking along the bank of a stream. We see from afar that he falls into the water. We run to his aid, but it's too late: he's dead by the time we pull him from the water. Looking at the spot where he fell in, we see a stone, and it seems obvious to conclude that the man stumbled over the stone, fell into the stream, and drowned. It could easily happen that this account would become widely accepted, that it would make sense to people. And it would be easy to imagine that this explanation would come down to posterity. But the real cause could have been completely different. A more careful analysis might have revealed that, right at the moment when the man reached the stone, he suffered a heart attack, fell into the water as a consequence, and then was pulled from the water dead. If the initial judgment had stood, and no one had investigated the events more thoroughly, then a false judgment would have dragged on throughout subsequent history, because it seemed so perfectly natural: the conclusion, namely, that the man had drowned after falling into the water. But the opposite could very well have been true: he didn't die because he fell into the water, but rather because he suffered a heart attack, and then fell into the water.

It's the easiest thing in the world for the real facts of the case to be turned upside-down. And indeed, as I've often pointed out, such upside-down explanations are commonplace in academic scholarship and scientific research.

There's an important lesson here for those of us who have dedicated ourselves with heart and soul to the anthroposophical movement: it's necessary not just that we learn from life, but also that we continually strive to learn the truth from life. We have to be constantly on the lookout for ways in which things that are untrue—illusions—can be transmitted not just via verbal accounts, but also by the seeming facts themselves. "Learning from life" should become the motto that guides all our striving. Otherwise it will be difficult for us actually to achieve what, among many other things, we want to achieve through our building:[1] vital, intimate participation[2] in the genesis of a historical epoch that's comparable to the unfolding of that earlier epoch, the transition from an older to a more "modern" era to which the Homeric epics refer.[3] Indeed, all the forms and the artistic and spiritual intentions embodied in our building are striving to effect a transition that's similar in a way to the transition from an older to a newer age that Homer narrates in his epics. We want to learn from life, to learn the truth from life.

There are so many opportunities to learn from life: all that's needed is the will to learn. Haven't we seen just such an opportunity over the last few days? Hasn't life provided us with a starting-point that's both deeply symptomatic and profoundly shattering?[4] Just consider how many of us walked past the intersection down the hill yesterday evening, or were close by; how many of us saw the overturned wagon; saw the wagon lying there; came to the lecture here; and quite obviously, quite naturally, were entirely unaware that anything else had happened besides a wagon tipping over. For hours that was the sole impression, for hours. But what was the truth? The truth was that within a human life an event had played out through which karma had spoken clearly. The truth was that a human life, which had unfolded so beautifully before our eyes, was concluded karmically in that moment. A human life was summoned back by spiritual powers, summoned back into spiritual worlds, because at certain times, for the benefit of evolution, these spiritual powers need human lives that have not been lived-out, and thus have forces left over that could have been expended on the physical plane, but now have been conserved for the spiritual worlds. We might even say: For those who have immersed themselves deeply in spiritual science, these events show clearly that we can look upon this as a life that the gods recalled unto themselves. We see clearly that, in order to bring about the fulfillment of this karma, the wagon was led to that spot, and then the wagon was overturned so that the karma of that particular individual might be fulfilled. It weighed heavily on our hearts at first, this event. And it's right we should feel that way. But we must also learn to feel in such events the sway of the wise powers that govern the world, even when those powers seem incomprehensible to us at first. And what better way to honor this human life, what better way for our souls to mark his passing, than to take this event as an occasion to learn the solemn lesson about karma that has been offered us in these days?

But we are all too readily inclined to neglect the lesson—even an all-too-transparent lesson such as this—the next time an occasion arises. We just forget it. That's why we have to let meditation—concentrated thinking—come to our aid. We have to try to come to terms with earthly events in the ways that are taught by spiritual science. We must never stop longing to accomplish this.

I would like to weave what I'll say today into the many other considerations we've raised in conjunction with our building, because it will serve to illustrate many points regarding aesthetics. We want to see what our building embodies as nothing less than a historical necessity. Right down into the individual forms, something should present itself to humanity that is really a historical necessity!

If we want to confront this task with deep seriousness, then our unceasing concern must be to gain from spiritual science the opportunity to reform our concepts and ideas. We have to gain better, higher, profounder, more solemn, more penetrating concepts and ideas about life than it would be possible to gain without anthroposophy.

That's the perspective from which I want to pose the fundamental question: What is history really, and what is this thing that people usually understand by the term "history"? Isn't what we usually call history actually like the story of the man wandering along the bank of the river who suffers a heart attack, dies, falls into the water, and is then remembered as having drowned in the water? Isn't history often something that stems from reports of this kind? Many, many historical reports are no better founded than this. Consider for example the possibility that somebody was passing by the crossroads on Wednesday between 8 and 9 p.m., and had no occasion to hear anything about the shattering event that took place there; hence he knew nothing beyond the fact that a wagon overturned there and that's what he would have reported. So it is with many historical reports. The matter of greatest import, lying beneath the ruins of the accounts as it were, remains completely hidden, stands completely apart from what we usually call history. Often we can go even further and say that external accounts, the documents, hinder our ability to recognize the true unfolding of historical events. That's especially the case if those documents depict the matter from one side or another, and there aren't any documents telling the other side of the story, or if those documents have been lost. And indeed that's the case in almost every historical epoch. Perhaps you think what I'm saying is just a hypothesis. But it isn't a hypothesis; to a great extent, the kind of history that's taught today is based upon such documents, which do more to hide the truth than to reveal it.

So the question might arise: Then how can we approach the unfolding of history? Well, in many different respects spiritual science has shown us the way, because anthroposophical historiography looks not to external documents, but rather to impulses from the spiritual world. And then of course we can't depict the external course of events in the same way that external history does. Instead we'll recognize everywhere the inner impulses that are at work. And spiritual scientists need to have the courage to foreground those inner impulses once they've been recognized, and to cleave to them, even if the external facts that have been transmitted appear to contradict them. We need to have the courage to believe in the truth of spiritual insight if we're to take our stand upon the ground of anthroposophy.

We can make the transition to this new kind of historiography by attempting to approach the mysteries of historical unfolding differently from the way in which it's usually done. Take all the extant documents relating to Italy from the thirteenth and fourteenth centuries; gather them all together, all the extant documents of the kind we employ so gladly in writing history. And if you assemble those documents, the history that results will be a tableau, a painting that corresponds much less to the truth than what results if you study what Dante and Giotto[5] created out of their inner lives. And if you add to that Scholasticism, all that has come down to us regarding the thoughts of the Scholastics, and if you attempt to rehearse in thought, to recreate what Dante, Giotto, and the Scholastics created, then you'll have a truer image of that epoch than you can attain by collating external records. Or if somebody had proposed to study the rebellion of the northern or central European Protestant spirit against the Catholicism of the South, what can we learn by studying the documents? What's important isn't to assimilate isolated facts; rather, what's important is that we empathize with the impulses that create, that rule, that weave within each epoch. We can truly understand the rebellion of the Protestant spirit against the spirit of Catholicism by studying Rembrandt, by coming to know Rembrandt in his unique way of painting. And many other such examples could be cited.

Moreover, it really is the case that we're often hindered by historical documents, if they are extant, rather than aided by them. Perhaps it might gladden the heart of a certain kind of historian who's very taken with documents if the life of Homer were well documented. And how elated such a historian would be if we had extensive documentation of the life of Shakespeare! And yet from a certain point of view we can say: Thank God that we have no such documents! Of course we shouldn't press this point of view, we shouldn't exaggerate it. But it's entirely valid to say that we should be thankful to history for having left us no documents on Homer or Shakespeare. I know, when I speak this way about both of these poets, someone could come and say something that would be true in a one-sided way, for, after all, a one-sided truth is still a truth. Someone could say: Well, then we should yearn for a time where we no longer have any external documents about Goethe! From a certain one-sided point of view, that perspective is entirely justified, but that's not the entire story.

It's true, is it not, that in the case of Goethe it's not just a hindrance, it's downright intrusive that we know what Goethe did as an individual not only from day to day, but sometimes from hour to hour. If you were to sit down and really picture to yourself what a soul such as Goethe was experiencing at a certain age when he uttered the fateful words:

> I have pursued, alas, philosophy,
> Jurisprudence, and medicine,
> And, help me God, theology,
> With fervent zeal through thick and thin,
> And here, poor fool, I stand once more,
> No wiser than I was before.[6]

then we really could yearn for the time when folks like Lewes[7] and all the rest no longer tell us what Goethe did all day, and when and where he wrote this or that verse. We really could say: what a hindrance it is for us in trying to follow the flight of Goethe's soul up to the time when he wrote the words "The sun contends in age-old fashion / With brother spheres in hymnic sound"[8] if we pick up Goethe's diaries and the collections of his letters in all their many volumes and read what it was that Goethe was doing at the time when he wrote down those sublime verses! What a hindrance it is to us!

But we're justified only to a limited extent in saying such a thing. Such a sentiment is entirely justified vis-à-vis Homer and Shakespeare, but it has only a limited validity with regard to Goethe. For Goethe himself wrote an autobiography entitled *Poetry and Truth*[9] in which he himself narrates his own life. It's integral to Goethe's personality that we know something of his life, because Goethe himself felt the need to make this confession through his book *Poetry and Truth*. Thus no one can say that the author of *Faust* stands before humanity in the same light as the author of the *Iliad* and the *Odyssey*. Hence you see that truths we've grasped from one perspective can't be extended to all cases. They can be brought to bear only upon the one specific case, upon something quite individual.

But really, we have to delve much more deeply into this whole issue. And that's what anthroposophy endeavors to do. Over and over—also in my previous lecture[10]—I've tried to show through a number of specific symptoms how it is that contemporary culture is striving for anthroposophy. In my book *The Riddles of Philosophy*[11] I sought to show how that is especially the case in philosophy. In volume two (which has just appeared and covers the history up to the present) you'll see how the development of philosophy is pressing on towards what I described in the final chapter as a "A Brief Outline of an Approach to Anthroposophy," how philosophy is tending in that direction. Of course that couldn't happen without some support from our Anthroposophical Society, for the public will probably understand very little of this book's inner structure.[12]

Let me add parenthetically a story about what can happen to a writer in our age, an episode that can only be described as "tasteless"! But when this lack of taste is aimed at a defenseless book, then it really becomes a sin against the rights that should prevail within cultural life. The second volume of *The Riddles of Philosophy* has 254 full pages, plus ten lines on page 255. When I received volume two from the publisher just this morning, I was shocked to discover that the publisher had shamelessly inserted an advertisement on the last page immediately beneath my text!

The book concludes with the words: "That is why this final chapter did not start by describing the way in which the soul speaks of the suprasensible when it stands within its realm. Quite to the contrary, an attempt was made to outline philosophically the tendencies resulting from the modern world conceptions, and it was shown how a pursuit of these innate tendencies leads the soul to the recognition of its own suprasensible nature."—And then immediately underneath the publisher has printed "Just appeared! J. Zangwill's complete *Ghetto Writings.* Authorized edition translated into German by Dr. Hanns Heinz Ewers."

That's the kind of shameless behavior authors have to suffer from publishers today, for we really have arrived at a point where nobody recognizes what good taste and spiritual life require.

Let me add that there was a passage in the preface where I wrote a few words attempting to justify why the book concludes with "A Brief Outline of an Approach to Anthroposophy." There you'll find the sentence: "The view expressed in this book tries to show that many situations arising from the solutions proposed by contemporary philosophy tend to recognize an element in the inner experience of the human soul that manifests itself in such a way that the exclusive claim of natural science can no longer deny that element its place in the modern worldview. If it is the philosophical conviction of the author of this book that the account of the final chapter deals with soul experiences ..." etc. Let me say expressly that the language here is something that was carefully crafted. Sometimes I have deliberated for hours about a single line. I wrote quite deliberately, "If it is the philosophical conviction of the author of this book ..." and then when I received the proofs, I found a note indicating that this turn of phrase was grammatically incorrect and hence the publisher would have to change it.[13] And so I had to engage in endless telephone conversations with the publisher, travel there by car and so forth. In the end it was printed as I intended, but I had to go through all that in order to ensure that the text I intended won out.

You see why we have to take seriously the need to bring anthroposophy right down into practical life. Not out of vanity, but because it's really needed—this is why we simply must create a "Philosophic-Anthroposophic Press."[14] We need to bring the ideas of anthroposophy right into life itself.

This is a symptom, if only a small one, of what's so characteristic of our time, and of its demands. If we succeed in speaking to our fellow human beings today through our new building in such a way that an aesthetic conscience is awakened, then something important will have been accomplished. I say this just as an aside.

As I said already, Goethe has to be regarded differently from Homer. But this difference arises for the same reason. Is there a better way to come to know Homer than through his poems, even though he lived not centuries but rather millennia ago? Isn't it true that we come to know him better through his poems than we could possibly do by means of all kinds of documents? Yes, the age of Homer was able to bring forth such works, through which the soul of Homer is laid bare. I could adduce countless examples; let's look at just one. Let's look at a passage that relates to the profoundest impulses underlying a transition that took place in evolution during the Homeric age. For we, too, are hoping to bring about such a transition when we yearn to transform our materialistic culture into an anthroposophical culture! We recall that Book One of *The Iliad* describes the opposition between Agamemnon and Achilles. Homer captures well the moods of Agamemnon and Achilles at Troy. We also recall that Book Two begins with the Greeks feeling they have camped all too long before the walls of Troy, and yearning to return home. And that Homer describes the situation in such a way that the gods are continually intervening and thereby act as the leading divine-spiritual powers. We find a description of Zeus intervening at the beginning of Book Two. Homer depicts how the gods above on Olympus and also the Greeks down below sleep peacefully—so peacefully that Herman Grimm,[15] that brilliant man, says you can just hear the snoring of Hera. Now at the beginning of Book Two, Homer continues:

> Now the great array of gods and chariot-driving men
> slept all night long, but the peaceful grip of sleep
> could not hold Zeus, turning it over in his mind...
> how to exalt Achilles?—how to slaughter
> hordes of Achaeans pinned against their ships?
> As his spirit churned, at last one plan seemed best:
> he would send a murderous dream to Agamemnon.[16]

So Zeus resolves to send Agamemnon a deceptive dream in the night.

> Calling out to the vision, Zeus winged it on:

Zeus speaks the following words to the dream:

> "Go, murderous Dream, to the fast Achaean ships
> and once you reach Agamemnon's shelter rouse him,
> order him, word-for-word, exactly as I command.
> Tell Atrides to arm his long-haired Achaeans,
> to attack at once, full force –
> now he can take the broad streets of Troy.
> The immortal gods who hold Olympus clash no more,
> Hera's appeals have brought them round and all agree:
> griefs are about to crush the men of Troy."

—so says Zeus to the dream—

> At that command
> the dream went winging off, and passing quickly
> along the fast trim ships, made for the king

and found him soon, sound asleep in his tent
with refreshing godsent slumber drifted round him.
Hovering at his head this vision rose like Nestor,
Neleus' son, the chief Agamemnon honored most.

So Zeus sends the dream down from Olympus to Agamemnon. He tasks the dream in the way that we've just heard. The dream approaches Agamemnon in the likeness of Nestor, one of the heroes who had also journeyed to Troy.

Inspired with Nestor's voice and sent by Zeus,
the dream cried out, "still asleep, Agamemnon?
The son of Atreus, that skilled breaker of horses?
How can you sleep all night, a man weighed down with duties?
Your armies turning over their lives to your command—
responsibilities so heavy. Listen to me, quickly!
I bring you a message sent by Zeus, a world away
but he has you in his heart, he pities you now …
Zeus commands you to arm your long-haired Achaeans,
to attack at once, full force—
now you can take the broad streets of Troy!
The immortal gods who hold Olympus clash no more,
Hera's appeals have brought them round and all agree:
griefs from Zeus are about to crush the men of Troy!
But keep this message firmly in your mind.
Remember—let no loss of memory overcome you
when the sweet grip of slumber sets you free."

So that's what happens: Zeus, who is guiding events, sends a dream to Agamemnon so that he'll rise up to perform a new deed. The dream appears in the likeness of Nestor, who is one of the heroes accompanying Agamemnon. So Agamemnon stands opposite the figure of Nestor, and Nestor, whom he knows well by physical appearance, tells him in the dream what he is to do. And moreover we're given to understand that Agamemnon gathers the chiefs before gathering the troops as a whole. And he narrates the dream to the chiefs, but he does so in the form in which he received it:

"Hear me, friends—
a dream sent by the gods has come to me in sleep.
Down through the bracing godsent night it came
like good Nestor in features, height and build,
the old king himself, and hovering at my head
the dream called on me: 'Still asleep, Agamemnon?
The son of Atreus ...'"

And so on. So Agamemnon tells the chiefs what the dream had said to him. None of the chiefs stands up; only Nestor, the real Nestor, stands up and says:

"Friends, lords of the Argives, O my captains!
If any other Achaean had told us of this dream
we'd call it false and turn our backs upon it.
But look, the man who saw it has every claim
to be the best, the bravest Achaean we can field.
Come—see if we can arm the Achaeans for assault."

Aren't we granted an endlessly profound insight into Homer's soul when, with the help of anthroposophy, we can know, we can see directly[17] that he's able to narrate such an episode? Didn't we describe a few days ago[18] how it is that our experiences in the spiritual world clothe themselves in images, that we have to interpret those images, and that we shouldn't allow ourselves to be deluded by those images? Homer, who spoke in an epoch when the old, atavistic clairvoyance was being lost, wanted to depict in the figure of Agamemnon a man who was still capable of receiving a kind of "epiphany"[19] of the old atavistic clairvoyance, who could be led through the old clairvoyance. Through dreams he's even led to plot military strategies. When we turn our attention to Homer and to what he depicts, we recall that the human soul then stood at the dawn of a new epoch. But we also come to realize something further. In the figure of Agamemnon, Homer depicts not only a human soul into whom the ancient clairvoyance still projects itself—and not just the very precise depiction of this clairvoyance—we're shown wonderfully, as though illumined by magic, the whole situation: Homer has Agamemnon describe explicitly that Nestor appeared to him—the same Nestor who is sitting right next to him and then speaks himself. Only a genuine poet can depict things so clearly.

But now let's move on. Agamemnon has gathered the chiefs and narrated his dream to them, Nestor has said that they should do what the dream commands. The armies gather, but Agamemnon speaks to the troops in a way that's very different from his dream experience. He says that it's wretched to camp before the walls of Troy for such a long time; we're longing to return home, we want to set sail, and so forth. That's what he says to them. He speaks in such a way that they're gripped by the strongest desire to run to their ships and sail home. And it takes all of Odysseus' rhetorical skill to bring it about that the armies return and besiege Troy in earnest.

Here we gain a real glimpse into Homer's soul. We see that in the character of Agamemnon he depicts the first human being who makes the transition from someone who's still guided by the old clairvoyance to one who acts on the basis of his own decisions. And so it is that he introduces us, with tremendous humor, first to the Agamemnon who speaks to the chiefs under the influence of the dream and then afterwards to the Agamemnon who overcomes that, who departs from the dream, and who, in speaking to the troops, reacts only to the impressions of outer events.

We see how Agamemnon grows beyond the previous epoch into the new age, where he stands at the apex of his own ego. How marvelous is Homer's depiction! What he wants to say to us is: This is how such a soul must make the transition in being led from the old clairvoyance to making his own decisions, to working out of human intelligence—out of what we call the "intellectual" or "mind soul,"[20] which we have ascribed to the ancient Greeks above all. And because Agamemnon, who's described as a transitional figure, crossing from the epoch of ancient clairvoyance into the new age, behaves erratically—first he speaks out of his clairvoyant dream, and then out of his own ego—for that reason, as Homer's plot proceeds he has to have recourse to the help of Odysseus, who acts solely out of intelligence, who makes decisions under the influence of the "intellectual soul." Here two distinct ages collide, and we can only admire how precisely Homer depicts that.

And now I ask you: Don't we come to know one aspect of Homer very well indeed when we understand this passage? Surely we do; with the help of this passage we come to know him in the way that we must if we wish to understand world history properly, and in a way we could never come to know him no matter how many external documents we possessed. But this is only one passage among many that we could cite. And if we did so, the figure of Homer would really stand before us; and we could come to terms with him in a way that would never have been possible if we had to do only with the personality known to us by means of external documents. Consider carefully what we know about Greek history. But if we approach Homer in this way, then we know Homer right down to the tip of his toes. And there were people who knew Homer in this way before philology interrupted so rudely and clouded the image. We get to know Socrates in this way through the depictions in Plato and Xenophon.[21] In the same way, we've come to know Plato himself and Aristotle; we've come to know even Phidias.[22] And if we have these figures before us, then an image of Greek antiquity arises upon the physical plane that we can expand with real intellectual integrity. To be sure, we need the help of anthroposophy. Just as the sun illuminates a landscape, anthroposophy illuminates Homer's lifelike[23] figures, and also those of Socrates and Plato; of Aeschylus, Sophocles, Phidias, and so forth.

But now let's try to contemplate Lycurgus[24] and Solon[25]; let's contemplate Alcibaides.[26] How do they stand before us when we look to Greek history? As pale as ghosts. Anyone who knows anything about human individuality is compelled to admit that they stand before us as mere specters. For the features that depict them are so abstract, so one-sided, that they come across as completely spectral. And the figures from later ages that have achieved historical existence only by way of external documents appear just as ghostly.

I'm saying all this so that I can really gather together a group of souls who will gradually attain the knowledge, understanding, and insight we need so that a new intervention, a new impulse can enter into our human evolution. And this is the case also with things that many people consider so well settled that to question them appears foolish. Before we can achieve this we still need many, many things.

In order to accomplish it, we need what might be called the will to penetrate into the world's true relationships; we need judgment in order to recognize that these true relationships are not always immediately visible on the surface. It's tremendously important for us to learn from life in this regard. To a very much greater degree than you might believe, error enters into human history, into human evolution, because people cling superficially to external states of affairs. In the way I described at the beginning of this lecture, those externalities can only hide the truth from us.

And particularly within the discipline of philosophy, I hope that the kind of depiction I have provided in volume two of *The Riddles of Philosophy* will make it possible for many people to see the real connection that exists between the philosophical foundation of the worldview as given in my book *The Philosophy of Freedom*[27] and the anthroposophical worldview as presented in my book *An Outline of Esoteric Science.*[28] If we attempt on the one hand to depict the spiritual worlds in the way in which they present themselves to clairvoyant cognition, then on the other side something has to complement the reception of these depictions. We have to complement those depictions with the knowledge that human beings don't just encounter truth immediately in the world: rather, the truth is something that they must first struggle to attain. Truth yields itself only to those who strive, who work; only to those who penetrate into the depths of things through their own activity. It's not revealed to those who just take superficial half-truths at face value. It's easy to say such a thing in the abstract, but over and over we find our souls are inclined to deviate from the striving for profounder insight that is actually intended.

Those of you who have tried to enter into anthroposophy with all the means it offers are already beginning to understand this. One example would be the way in which the harmony of the columns and the motifs, together with everything else in our building, attempts to provide the soul with means to transcend the appearances of immediate perception. If the soul begins to experience what lives in the forms of our building, then the forms themselves will disappear from the soul, and by means of what is living in the forms—the language of the forms—the soul will find its path outward into the wide spheres of the spiritual world. Then our building shall achieve its purpose. But in order to find that path, we still have much to learn from life itself.

My dear friends! Isn't it ultimately a remarkable experience of karma that all of us who have gathered here for the purpose of building the Goetheanum were able to share in the shattering experience? Didn't the death of Theo Faiss reveal to us the real connection between karma and seemingly outward happenstance? With the help of everything we have experienced up to this point in our anthroposophical striving we can begin to understand that human beings taken from us too soon, who have not experienced the cares and the many tribulations of life, and who crossed the threshold again still untouched by life—that such lives become forces within the spiritual world that develop a relationship to the whole of human life, that exist in order to affect the whole of human life. I have often said that the earth is not just a vale of woe into which we have been sent by the higher worlds as a kind of punishment. No, the earth is there as a school for us. When a human life ends early, when a human soul undergoes only a brief schooling, then the forces that otherwise would have been expended upon the physical body are liberated, so that they can stream down from the spiritual world and continue working. Anthroposophy gives us conviction not just with regard to the immortality of the soul, and to its journey through the spiritual world; we also learn about the persistence of the working of such spiritual force when someone is torn from their physical body as was this good lad who has been taken from us on the physical plane. And we honor and celebrate his physical demise with proper dignity if we learn in the ways I have described from this and many other things that we've experienced over the last few days; only if we learn very, very much. We learn to experience anthroposophy with feeling and sensibility. And then, when we are confronted by such a case, we look up in the right way into those spheres into which the soul of the child has been delivered, the child whose physical body we returned to Mother Earth today.

The verse that many anthroposophists are reciting for human

beings who are sacrificing their individualities[29] can be spoken, with a slight modification, also to such souls who have left the earthly plane. For such souls also receive the entreaty that we speak. This entreaty is valid for the living and it is valid for the dead. And if we are convinced that the soul has already departed the bodily sheaths, then we speak the mantra that most of those present today surely know, but with a slight change, with the little change I will make in sending it on now after dear, good Theo—Theo whose soul lives on in celestial spheres as a celestial being:

> Spirit of his soul, active guardian
> May thy pinions bring
> The entreating love of our souls
> To the celestial being given over to your protection;
> So that, united with thy power
> Our entreaty might stream in aid
> To the soul it is lovingly seeking.[30]

Lecture 2

Dornach, October 18, 1914

Our building in Dornach should be appreciated by those in our circles for the universality of its style. In order for that to happen, our friends need to transform into a new sensibility everything that has come to our souls over the years from anthroposophical research. Then our new, inner sensibility will teach us how to view the forms of our building as a script that's universal, and hence filled with a wide range of meanings.[31]

In my last talk here I pointed out ways in which we can grab hold of[32] a universal sense for human evolution. I pointed out that we can come to recognize Homer as a transitional figure; how we can sense in him the transition from ancient times, in which all aspects of human evolution and human culture were founded upon a certain clairvoyance, to the time in which we ourselves live and into which there shone the first glimmer of the Mystery of Golgotha,[33] which is meant to emanate into the future.

I said that in Agamemnon and Achilles, Homer has created figures through whom he showed how the old, clairvoyant forms of human knowledge were evolving, changing into new ways of feeling, thinking, perceiving, willing, and also acting.

Fundamentally speaking, everything humanity has experienced since the blossoming of the fourth post-Atlantean epoch,[34] the age of Greece and Rome, can be understood only if we grasp how it rests upon the foundation of the ancient cultures of clairvoyance.[35] This is true of everything that has happened since, even of that which the various cultures are striving to achieve today.

Of course there are many new attainments within the fourth post-Atlantean epoch, as well as in the portion of the fifth post-Atlantean epoch[36] that we have already experienced. But anyone who is sensitive to its fundamental thrust can feel clearly what is still alive within the fourth and fifth post-Atlantean epochs as a holdover from ancient times.

It's not so easy to recognize immediately this ancient legacy as the foundation of human evolution beneath the superficial events of the historical record. But you can see it if you're open to looking a bit into what holds sway more or less unconsciously within human nature, and thereby has found its way into recent history. Then you can see everywhere how the people of the fifth post-Atlantean epoch are suffused with it; in their nerves and in their blood they bear within them legacies from the first post-Atlantean epoch, the Ancient Indian; from the second, the Ancient Persian; from the third, the Egypto-Chaldean epoch;[37] and especially from the fourth, the Greco-Roman epoch. All that has carried over into our time. Everything that came to pass during these cultural epochs, all that humanity worked to attain, is less visible in the external historical records. But you can feel your way into it and sense it by contemplating the inner nature of the historical actors themselves, their mentalities. We can empathize with the ways they must have thought and felt—and I mean "must." Human beings of the fifth cultural epoch, in which we live, are such that in our nerves, our blood, our etheric[38] and astral[39] bodies something is contained that is an inheritance from ancient times. It lives within us. It lives within us as a feeling, as a fundamental instinct.[40] And we've added to this inheritance what descends to us from higher worlds.

We live in a time when the human individuality or I is developing, in an age in which intellectuality directed toward the external world sets the tone for culture, at a time when exoteric philosophy must reign. Hence there is little understanding for what comes down from above, from the wise guidance of the spiritual worlds, and enters into our human impulses within the physical world.

And if we want to capture—let's say, capture for our dynamic feeling in a visual motif[41]—the situation of humanity during the fifth post-Atlantean epoch against the larger backdrop of the evolution of consciousness as a whole, then we can indicate it in a few strokes by choosing *this* motif. [Steiner draws on the blackboard the lower half of Fig. 1.] What this motif represents is a force that really is directed upwards from below; it makes visible for our feeling all of the forces that we bear within our blood and nerves, in our etheric and astral bodies. These are forces that first evolved during the period immediately preceding the first post-Atlantean epoch.[42]

And then we can signify our own human intuition as a force working downward from above, in an impulse flowing down from above. This force comes to us from the spiritual world, but it is weaker than the forces we bear within us as a holdover from older eras. [Steiner draws on the blackboard the upper half of the motif in Fig. 1.]

FIG. 1[43]

Anthroposophical research provides a thread that can guide us to an understanding of the context within which we live. We need only think of the ways in which anthroposophical research has striven to recognize how the impulses at work within the leading cultures of the fifth post-Atlantean epoch manifest themselves within the various faculties of the human soul. We need only think of the ways in which the peoples who inhabit the Italian and Spanish peninsulas—as peoples, not as individuals; that is something I've explained here already repeatedly—how those peoples assimilate into their cultures everything connected with the sentient soul[44] such that everything we feel to be of the nature of the sentient soul lives primarily within these peoples who inhabit the Italian and Spanish peninsulas. These peoples developed further in a special way the central process that is indicated by this motif [the lower portion of Fig. 1]. In a certain sense, they manifest more concretely, with sharper contours, what lives within the impulses of the blood and nerves, the etheric and astral bodies, in the way that I previously described. We might say that everything carried over from primordial times comes to expression in these peoples in a way that gives a more definite contour[45] to the forces striving upward from below. There is something that's still inorganic, a kind of bare dynamism about this motif; it attempts to give some sense of the first stirrings of the fifth post-Atlantean epoch.

If we want to focus on what's special about the peoples of the Italian and the Spanish peninsulas, then we have to be clear that they cultivate the impulses in the blood, in the nerves, in the etheric and astral bodies, in ways that are more differentiated and concrete. They do this in order to move consciously toward the future, but they do this by employing the force of the past. Briefly, we indicate the special impetus rising up from below within these peoples by expanding this motif [the bottom half of Fig. 1], shaping it such that it opens like a blossom facing upwards. And then above, we form a motif that tries to give at least some sense of the capacity for understanding what comes down from above in this era. [Over the next several minutes, Steiner gradually sketches out Fig. 2 on the blackboard.]

FIG. 2

These cultures show little engagement with the influences indicated by this motif here [the upper part of Fig. 2], but they drink deep draughts from the well of the forces carried over by the sentient soul from the past. They carry over all the mysteries of the older forms—or we could say, all the mysteries of the ancient artistic iconographies.[46] We have to show this [in the drawing] by allowing everything that impresses itself upon the forms out of earlier times to come down from above like a renewed gift. Everything that lives within the nature of these peoples rests upon a column, as it were, so that it is expressed by this motif[47] that I've sketched on the board [Fig. 2].

Anthroposophy looks for confirmation of its insights by surveying the historical record. And we have to survey the external historical records if we want to take up anthroposophy in the right way. But first of all we must lay upon our hearts and our souls that which anthroposophy says and only afterwards pose the question: Is what anthroposophy says something that actually exists in the world? Has it been realized there? Which is to say: If anthroposophy were to seek confirmation in the way just indicated, then we would have to find what lives predominantly within the sentient soul within the external culture of those peoples; we would have to find within the cultures of the peoples of the fifth post-Atlantean epoch a kind of resurrection[48] of something that was already present in earlier times, and to which all the aforementioned peoples of the sentient soul give their characteristic stamp. Hence we would have to find a recapitulation of the Egypto-Chaldean epoch, but born anew, in a form suited to the modern age.[49]

So what was it that lived within the souls of the people of the Egypto-Chaldean age? It was a deep original participation of the external world[50] in keeping with the character of the sentient soul—participation in the stars. They experienced their relationship to the fixed stars and the stars that wander, the planets, as an innate, truly sublime astrology.[51] They looked out into the edifice of the cosmos and found within the language of the stars the secrets of their own inner lives.

What we should expect to find is that the first part of the culture of the fifth post-Atlantean epoch recapitulates inwardly, from the soul outward, what lay within this culture of the sentient soul. Hence we could expect, if the indications of anthroposophy are a genuine guide for us, that something would emerge within the native communities[52] of the Italian and Spanish peninsulas which, on the one hand, expresses the sentient soul quality of the Egypto-Chaldean epoch, and on the other hand corresponds to the inward turn that was effected by the Mystery of Golgotha. We would expect to encounter something that revived an analogue of[53] the old, spiritual astrology, but now applied it to the inner life, to the human soul. When we contemplate the simple forms of Egypto-Chaldean culture, we would expect to find special, blossom-like forms emerging, expressing in this motif [Fig. 2, bottom] the upward-striving impulses manifested by human beings, and in the motif above it, that which rays down from the stars (which is to say, from the spiritual world). There would have to be something within the culture of the Southern peoples which represented an "ensouled" culture, a revival of Egypto-Chaldean-Babylonian astrology that now has been internalized, filled with soul.

My dear friends, it's obvious what must come to mind as a perfect example of the tendencies I was just describing: I mean of course Dante's *Divine Comedy*.[54] Dante was the great spirit who "psychologized"[55] the older Egypto-Chaldean age, who brought it back to life inwardly and filled it with soul.

It will be easy for you to designate the qualities within the fifth post-Atlantean epoch that are connected with the fundamental, primeval impulses of prehistoric times as *saturnine*.[56] [Steiner writes the word "saturnine" on the blackboard, adding it to Fig. 1.] The fundamental trait shared by everything that connects the cultures of the fifth post-Atlantean epoch with older cultures is this saturnine quality. The saturnine quality works its way up out of the fundamental impulses of the human soul and then receives from above impulses through which precisely the culture of the sentient soul, the culture of the intellectual or mind soul,[57] and of the I can germinate.

And it is likewise easy to designate the next motif [Fig. 2] as *solar*. [The word "solar" is added to Fig. 2 on the blackboard.] I just referred to the "solar quality" of an important impulse of the Latin-Italian culture, as one sees it in Dante. We need only add that Italy is the motherland of all forms,[58] of everything sunlike that needs to approach humanity through the sentient soul. We might even expect that a thinker with a very specific character would need to step forth within this culture, someone who spoke out of his unconscious impulses in such a way that it reminds us of this solar quality. It would be entirely natural to find such a thing following the guiding thoughts of anthroposophy.

We can imagine for example a philosopher who might have remained unclear in his own soul regarding the philosophical impulse that he brought, but felt it and allowed it to rule him nevertheless. A philosopher who might say: The political life of the state must be arranged in such a way that the sun-like qualities of culture irradiate this outer political life as well. It was possible for that feeling to live in a philosopher such that he spoke of the sun-like quality of this culture, even as it manifests within the outer, social concourse among human beings. We should not be surprised to find such a thing. Campanella wrote a philosophical treatise that he entitled *The City of the Sun*.[59]

You will gain ever greater conviction that everything, every detail, is in harmony with what anthroposophy draws down out of spiritual heights, and that if you really want to understand life, there is no other way to do that than to illuminate it with the results of anthroposophy.

Moving on, we come to the culture that anthroposophical research has led us to call the culture of the intellectual or mind soul. This faculty was developed during the fifth post-Atlantean epoch in the region of present-day France. To this culture fell the task of taking up what comes down from above in a more concrete sense than was the case earlier, especially at any point in the unfolding of Italian-Spanish culture, and thereby to refine and elaborate further the intellectual or mind soul, to make it blossom. The right kind of motif to signify this culture would have to be characterized as follows.

Here [Fig. 3, top half of left side] is a motif for what comes down from above, and here [Fig. 3, bottom half of left side] a motif for what comes up from below. The culture of the intellectual or mind soul, which had previously been present only *in abstracto*, is now set forth *in concreto*, and shows itself to be especially well suited to take up what comes down from above.

FIG. 3

Anyone who enters empathetically into the inmost qualities of French culture will feel that it really is especially inclined to take up again what carries over from Greece and Rome. They will feel that the fourth post-Atlantean epoch has arisen again within French culture. We could say that Greece and Rome trickle down into French culture and suffuse it, like a liquid trickling down into a chalice.

Thus, Spanish and Italian culture give way to French culture, but in such a way that Greek culture rises up within the French. I doubt you can find a form that captures the transition from Spanish and Italian culture into French culture better than this motif [Fig. 3, right], which we have allowed to become enclosed, separated on the left and on the right by these lines.

Anyone who doubts whether the insights of anthroposophy are confirmed by historical evidence can readily find such confirmation by studying the actual relationships. Needless to say, the only way to form a proper judgment regarding such relationships is to contemplate the facts without preconceived notions.

In our time we have to stress this over and over again, because today everyone wants to pass judgment on everything while ignoring the facts. Learning the facts is difficult, after all: we have to learn them by coming to terms with life itself. But if anyone wanted to gain insight into the entirely characteristic way in which the mentality of the Greeks streamed into the mentality of French culture, I would recommend studying how the figure of Oedipus was introduced into French poetry, how the Oedipus of Sophocles comes to life again in the Oedipus tragedies by Corneille[60] and Voltaire.[61] Right down into the smallest details, you can find confirmation of what I have just asserted. And it's not just in this one single example that you'll find it confirmed; many examples could be adduced. But you have to approach them with a truly open mind.

It's a sad fact that in most editions of Corneille's works you won't find his tragedy *Œdipe*, and that in the case of Voltaire this work is no longer well regarded. But anyone who studies these works will find that the transformation of Oedipus by Corneille and Voltaire signifies the rebirth of the Greek epoch within French culture.

You'll find in the version by Sophocles that he has imbued his heroic tragedy with the remnants of the old clairvoyance that still lived within the Greco-Latin epoch, while in the versions by Corneille and Voltaire everything has become very simple, entirely a matter of the human soul. In making this judgment, we have to disregard completely whether the Oedipus of Sophocles is more congenial to us than the later versions. We have to concentrate solely on the transformation that has occurred. Of course we must note that this transformation tends in modern times toward engendering Oedipus out of the personal nature of the human soul alone.

As I said, we have to disregard what we find personally uncongenial. And so we're disregarding that. But in the process we can nevertheless indicate quite objectively that in the versions of Corneille and Voltaire something new has entered into the literature on Oedipus. In Sophocles, the figure of Oedipus appears to us as though bound up in a universally human destiny that we can describe only with the words that the poet himself uses to describe such a monumental, gigantic destiny: destiny raises humans up by crushing them. The aura of magic that emanates from the Oedipus of Sophocles arises because we can sense in this tragedy how the spiritual worlds guide the destinies of whole peoples.[62] The spiritual worlds intervene in human destiny in such a way that destiny remains opaque to humanity, we cannot penetrate it, and the suffering that the gods bring to humanity may appear to us to be the bitterest injustice.

We can imagine that every Greek had some sense of the inscrutability of destiny, within which even the will of the gods is inscrutable. At any moment any individual can be struck by the same destiny as this Oedipus. Destiny remains inscrutable.

This aura of magic that emanates from Sophocles' Oedipus tragedy has become something eminently personal in Corneille and Voltaire. It was Corneille who effected the transition; it was Voltaire who gave it full expression. For in Voltaire's Oedipus drama we have a configuration that would have been unthinkable in antiquity: the Prince Philoctetes, the friend of the family who turns the conjugal pair into a love triangle. Jocasta already knew Philoctetes before her marriage; the affair continued until she became an interesting widow and then married her own son, Oedipus. Those are all personal relationships of a kind that are impossible in ancient drama.

But we can go further; we can attempt to understand everything that was animating the great French poets, and we will find that the assimilation of the Greek element is clearly evident, both in literature and in French poetics. For we know after all how Lessing[63] undertook to study the ways in which French literature assimilated into its poetics an aesthetic principle from the Greek classics; we know after all how the classical "unities" of time, place, and action[64] play a role in Corneille, Racine, and Voltaire.

It's impossible to understand French classical literature without focusing on this emanation of the spirit of ancient Greece that found its way into French literature. And if we want to see the guidelines that anthroposophy gives us realized very vividly in this culture, we can accomplish that by posing the question: Where is it that the essence of this French culture actually confronts us most distinctively? Where is French culture unsurpassed? Where does it achieve its culmination? To be sure, we have to summon up all the objectivity we can in order to answer these questions properly, and people are little inclined toward objectivity, especially in our time. But anyone who considers the matter objectively would have to conclude that the summit of French culture is to be found in the comedies of Molière.[65] For all that Corneille and Racine and indeed all of modern French culture have attained, the works of Molière have reached a degree of perfection that cannot ever be attained again. And even if some nation came to believe that the same thing could be attained out of the spirit of a different culture, then the only objective reply would be: Certainly works that are equally perfect in a different way, and even things that are more perfect, but not in this way. If one were to assert that the peculiar character of Molière—the character of Molière as born from the intellectual or mind soul—could arise again, or even that an echo of it could be attained, that would be a mistake. In Molière we see the culmination of the essence of the culture that wells forth from the intellectual or mind soul.

Molière's comedies are comedy-itself,[66] and it's impossible to understand their spiritual import unless you know that the intellectual soul reigns within them—playing itself out in such a uniquely characteristic way. Everything that arises within human evolution reveals itself in its purely archetypal form only once. Just as we never will be 18 or 25 years old twice during a single lifetime, there never will be another Molière.

All of that can be captured aesthetically in this motif [Fig. 3].

My dear friends, let me digress here for a moment by referring to the things I said in my cycle of lectures on the folk-souls,[67] specifically the European folk-souls of the fifth post-Atlantean epoch. Now we can pose new questions in the same style, questions that are connected with our discussion of Central European culture as the culture of the I.

If it's true that Central European culture is the culture of the I, then its relationship to the other cultures we have discussed will be similar to the relationship within the human being between the I and the sentient soul, the intellectual or mind soul, and the consciousness soul. Here too the results of anthroposophical research would have to provide our guidelines. If Italian culture represents what's assimilated by the sentient soul, then it would need to stand in a certain relationship to the culture of the I, to the culture of Central Europe. That is to say, Central European culture, which exerts its influences predominantly through the I, would have to be predisposed to delve down into the sentient soul, to play itself out, to allow itself to be fertilized by it in the same way that this happens within the I and sentient soul of individual human beings.

Let's consider the relationship between the I and the sentient soul. The I, which contains the impulses of actual inwardness, must delve down into the sentient soul; otherwise it is not fertilized by everything that the external world in all its forms can exert upon it. We humans have to delve down over and over into our sensations. The I needs to grapple with the impulses coming up through the senses. So we might expect that the denizens of the I-culture of Central Europe would seek a vital connection with the culture of the sentient soul in the South; that they would seek to expand outward politically, but also with regard to higher spiritual matters.

Then go and look up the history of the Hohenstaufens;[68] look up the history that unfolded in Central Europe among the Hohenstaufens and the Guelphs and the Ghibellines.[69] Look up all the stories about the Saxons' and the Hohenstaufens' continual campaigns against Italy. Study the whole life of Central Europe in relation to Italy, and you will see exactly the same relationship as in the life that unfolds between the sentient soul and the I.

Moreover, we can expect that the I by its very nature should call forth out of our inner life as human beings forms that appear in the history of art. What we would expect to arise out of the I would be gnarled forms, forms that are typical of the ways in which the I shapes things. And we find such forms in Holbein and in Dürer.[70] But in the case of Dürer we find them only after his stay in Italy,[71] where his art was enriched by encountering the Italian culture of the sentient soul.

If we move on to more recent centuries, we find the same phenomenon everywhere. From Goethe's Italian journey, through Cornelius and Overbeck,[72] right up to today—everywhere we see the culture of the I trying to come to terms with the culture of the sentient soul.

All this cultural traffic between Central Europe and Italy is an image of the unfolding relationship between the individual human I and sentient soul. When we investigate them right down into the smallest details, outer events provide strong confirmation of what is to be found in the body of our anthroposophical research.

Now let's consider the relationship that exists between the I-aspect of the soul and the intellectual or mind soul. There we should expect to see the relationship that unfolds within the human soul between the I and the intellectual or mind soul emerging within outer life as well.

The relationship between the I and the sentient soul is such that the I delves down uncritically when it allows itself to be enriched by the culture of the sentient soul.

As we would expect, the relationship between the I and the intellectual soul is more intellectual, an encounter that is more of the head. For the intellectual or mind soul is the faculty[73] of the human soul that avails itself of thinking. Please try to develop an idea[74] of this faculty by studying the descriptions in my book *Theosophy*. It's simultaneously the faculty of the human soul that's the proper element of the I, and the faculty with which the I must come to terms for its own sake.

Hence we must expect an intimate relationship between the culture of the intellectual soul and the culture of the I. It's impossible to imagine a better representative of this relationship within the human being—it's obvious that one can't, but let's say it anyway because it will help draw our attention to what is most important—it's impossible to imagine a better representative than the Central European philosopher Leibniz[75] and his relationship to French culture. The quality of Leibniz's thinking is preeminently Central European. All of the external influences upon him—for example the influence of Giordano Bruno,[76] who is such an archetypal bearer of the Italian sentient soul—Leibniz translated into Central European,[77] as it were. But Leibniz wrote in French, and much in his philosophy takes on forms required by the French language.

And we also see the culture of the I grappling with the culture of the intellectual or mind soul when we consider the remarkable polemics in Lessing's *Hamburg Dramaturgy*.[78] We see the struggle between the ideal that Lessing is striving to achieve and the Greek spirit within French culture, from which Lessing wants to liberate himself. Lessing polemicizes; he grapples within his intellect. That is a precise image of the struggle between the I and the intellectual or mind soul. We begin to understand Lessing's *Hamburg Dramaturgy* in the right way only when we view it from this perspective.

And here's another factor that people are inclined to overlook today: the various forms that external relationships within Central Europe have taken are connected in many regards with the ambitions of Prussia. Who wouldn't connect the ambitions of the Prussian state with the figure of Frederick the Great? And yet when we look at him we have to conclude that he was devoted to France with every fiber of his being, and that he assimilated many things from French culture. He said that he considered Voltaire to be a greater individuality than Homer. He saw German culture as something that was still half barbaric. He strove for culture by reaching out for everything French, and in that way Frederick the Great can be seen as an archetypal political representative of the culture of the I. Many aspects of Prussia cannot be understood without taking into consideration Frederick the Great's encounter with French culture.

All the aforementioned phenomena shed light upon the culture of the I, in the same way that insight into the intellectual or mind soul sheds light upon the I within the individual human being, as I noted already in my book *Theosophy*.

It is devoutly to be wished that people would consider the real underpinnings of current events before making all kinds of pronouncements. Then at least some people would recognize the shocking lack of judgment manifested by contemporary journalism, with all its emptiness and frivolity and its dissipated cynicism.

If we attempt to proceed further within human evolution, the evolution that is unfolding within the fifth post-Atlantean epoch, then of necessity we arrive at the progression in this motif [transition from Fig. 3 to Fig. 4].

Fig. 4

This progression is able to express itself through this motif because the influences descending from above into the culture of the intellectual soul build it up powerfully. The result is a certain closure vis-à-vis the Spirit,[79] which can be indicated by allowing a form that closes itself off to flow into the progression of this motif above it.

Thus while that which descends from above streams into the fifth post-Atlantean epoch in a way that is still concrete and gives to that age its entirely characteristic stamp, there is a certain sense in which here it closes itself off vis-à-vis this streaming influence. We encounter the preparations for the culture of the consciousness soul, which must be especially characteristic of the fifth post-Atlantean epoch. Whereas Italian culture is a revival of the Egypto-Chaldean epoch, and whereas the culture of the intellectual or mind soul (which reached its culmination in the Greco-Roman Age, the fourth post-Atlantean epoch, which still veiled the consciousness soul) flowed into French culture, now we arrive at something that is especially characteristic of the fifth post-Atlantean epoch, within which humanity is left entirely to its own devices.

What is the relationship to the external world that this culture has to develop? Left to its own devices, humanity becomes an "onlooker," and hence, because humanity has developed this relationship to the world, it becomes able to look on from the outside, and thereby see deeply into the configuration of beings,[80] into their organism and mechanism, in order to construct them from within, so that they stand there in the way that nature itself created them. A culture of "onlookers," a culture of sharp-witted spectatorship and delving down into beings is what we find there, so that the depictions are like those of an outside observer. When this culture reaches its culmination, what form will it take?

We need name only one name: Shakespeare. He is great, unsurpassed as an observer of the world, and Shakespeare's works are inconceivable in any earlier culture, but also inconceivable in any culture later than his own.

When I undertook to depict the characteristic English philosopher in the first edition of my *Worldviews of the Nineteenth Century*[81] fifteen years ago, I didn't resort to the interpretation I just described, but already then I was seeking some such telling expression. You can find it in the second volume of my book *The Riddles of Philosophy*. I was looking for a phrase that would capture John Stuart Mill, something that would express the fundamental character of his philosophy. And I decided I had to choose the word "onlooker," someone who "looks on the world."[82] And indeed that's what we find in outer historical events by following the guidelines of anthroposophy.

And now if we pose the other question again, the question of the confrontation of the I with the consciousness soul, well, then we see something very characteristic. As we would expect, much that the I seeks comes to it via the consciousness soul, because the chief task of the consciousness soul is to nurture and cultivate the I. We would expect to see many things flowing from the consciousness soul into the I, and yet, because the I wants to preserve and protect its autonomy, it has to mount resistance against many things as well.

It's grand to watch how modern physics is given its characteristic stamp by Newton, and then how, through Goethe, the Central European culture of the I rebels against the culture of the consciousness soul. Have a look at Goethe's *Color Theory*:[83] it's magnificent to see how he rises up against Newton there. This tension mirrors the inner conflict between the I and the consciousness soul.

In Central Europe much is rooted in the I, which—as with, for example, Jakob Böhme[84]—expresses itself as something spiritual. In his case, the I often fails to find the right words, whereas the consciousness soul does find the words; it finds what is outwardly effective. We should look to Goethe in order to see how it is that Central Europe's culture of the I unfolds in its natural progression[85] of upward striving. Just how it is that Goethe finds what can be termed the "culture of the I" is not immediately obvious, however; I am referring to his profound theory of the way in which evolution unfolds naturally from the simplest to the most highly developed being. Goethe's own contemporaries didn't understand it. Then along comes Darwin, who gives birth from out of the consciousness soul to the same thing that Goethe had developed from out of the I, and everyone in the world understands it. Even the culture of the I understands it.[86]

It is only possible to point to the image of genuine human evolution by recognizing these true relationships in light of the guidance provided by anthroposophy. What lives within human evolution unfolds its life culture by culture, as though resting upon the primordial columns of the archetypal laws of humanity.[87]

Following these motifs, we can sense the progression from the basically saturnine character of the fifth post-Atlantean epoch to the solar character of the culture of the Italian and Spanish South, which still conceals the lunar quality within itself, and which develops further into the Mars culture that unfolds upon the British Isles [Fig. 4]. And the only way we can come to understand what we must understand—the harmony of the post-Atlantean cultures as in a chorus—is by gaining a sense for the peculiar qualities of these post-Atlantean cultures. Thus all the post-Atlantean cultures sound together like a great chorus. If anthroposophy is alive within us, then all our feeling should flow from knowledge of human evolution.

We should strive to form a cupola over our heads, a cupola that rises up above the motifs that we sense and feel, that approach our soul when we follow the progress of human evolution. The cupola will reveal to us how human beings—how the various nations—collaborate, and how that is in turn an image of the collaboration of the various inner faculties within our human nature itself. If we enter our building with a cultivated mind and heart[88] it will have an effect upon our souls. For in erecting this building we have sought to disregard everything having to do with the individual human personality. In every line and in every motif, we have sought to render not the individual human personality, but rather what the spiritual worlds reveal when they want to mold their activity[89] into distinct forms that allow humans to understand its meaning.

Humanity is still far, very far indeed, from having transformed into a living sensibility the ideas about which I have spoken again today. In order for that to be accomplished, anthroposophy will have to spread more and more widely. And we will need to cultivate ever greater understanding for a new style of building that is connected to the mysteries of the cosmos[90]—a style such as we have attempted to create with our building. Naturally our building can represent only a feeble beginning, nothing more. But within the unconscious of this or that person, to a greater or a lesser degree, we can already see rising up something that will give us the materials we need to fashion an understanding of the ways in which the various cultures, the living cultures of the fifth post-Atlantean epoch, harmonize with each other.

And so it is that we can rise up in the face of many things, even at this time that is so full of suffering, and greet them, because the events of today must be our occasion to seek out within them something that has great promise for the future. We need to create *an energetic culture of peace*[91]—not idle talk of peace, but the real peace that can arise only out of a concrete, mutual understanding of the various individual cultures.

We are very far from realizing this anthroposophical ideal; too much of what we do is actually the product of a merely egotistical identification with this or that national culture.[92] But meanwhile we must greet with a measure of satisfaction any attempt to understand what really binds the various cultures together, for that alone is the source of genuine creativity.

And so despite the many events that bring us such great pain, we can also recall other voices that are heartening because they show it's possible also for those outside our immediate circle to honor the insights of anthroposophy. It's true, nowadays very few people want to know anything about anthroposophy. And yet, just as I showed how there's an unconscious longing for anthroposophy in Herman Grimm,[93] I could show you something similar in others among our contemporaries.

Let me adduce just one of those many voices here. When the students at a Central European university were caught up in the war, some of them drafted and some of them remaining at home, a professor at that university spoke words that are heartening, words that deserve to become widely known. Although they were spoken without knowledge of anthroposophy, they reveal impulses of real hope and longing for the kind of mutual intercourse among the nations that must arise in the future. He said: "You will experience that nothing prepares a cultivated soul for an intimate experience of beauty so much as the trials of heroic action. And you will experience that nothing rouses and steels you for new trials, and that nothing binds soul to soul so intensely as the holy kingdom of beauty. Yes, even if a hatred among nations must remain behind as the most terrible consequence of this war, a hatred greater than any ever seen, even within that enmity, *you* will not forget to feel love for the better angels of the enemy. You are fighting the good fight for the truth. You do not need the vile incitements and the slanders of infected minds. Among the great minds of German culture you will receive Shakespeare as a guest, for, as he is one of us, much English thought belongs now irrevocably to our culture. You will remember the noble striving of the French spirit for the finest aesthetic culture. You will remember that in our own time Russia received its Homer and Shakespeare in Tolstoy and Dostoyevsky. To be sure, the Russian state often brought to both these greatest sons of Russia only suffering, and sometimes inhuman persecution. What would they say about the events of our day! But through them there speaks unforgettably, in blessed fervor and simplicity, the eternal gospel of the people of God, the kingdom of succoring human love. The meaning of the war will be found in the peace to which it leads. As warriors, bear the high ideal of the coming peace within you, so that hatred among nations might nevertheless lead to a new kingdom of love. We are most profoundly and truly German when we love everything with a human countenance, and when we see the quality of each national culture as a unique configuration of humanity and a revelation of God. The kingdom of loving human understanding is the kingdom of the German spirit."

These words were spoken by Professor Eugen Kühnemann on August 18, 1914.[94] He imparted these words to students heading off to war. It is a heartening expression at this great moment, in which we are experiencing so much that is disheartening and heavy. These words reveal a great understanding for Shakespeare, who is also one of us, so that English thoughts are part of our intellectual life, as are the fruits of French culture. He highlights the meaning of Tolstoy and Dostoyevsky within modern spirituality. Better this than what one hears so often today on the other side!

May just this attitude persist in our time! And perhaps our friends [from other countries] can help make it known that such an attitude can also be found over here, and—let me stress this—it is not as rare over here as one might have been led to believe.

Let's conclude our deliberations for today, and meet again tomorrow at 7 o'clock. Then we'll follow the further progress of evolution—via the cultures of Central Europe and Russia—as expressed in our columns.

Fig. 1

Fig. 2

Fig. 3

Fig. 4

Lecture 3

Dornach, October 19, 1914

If we continue to contemplate the evolution of the European cultures in the fifth post-Atlantean epoch, then we arrive at the cultural epoch that I came to represent with the following motif [Fig. 5] when I was working on our columns:

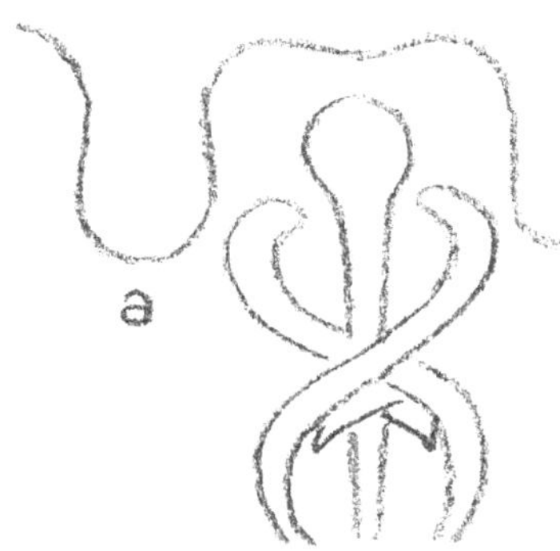

Fig. 5

All of you know this motif from our columns. What I would like you to consider especially is that it's accompanied by a "drop-like" motif here above [a]. You can feel how this motif is justified if you look to Central European, post-Atlantean culture. I say explicitly *Central European* post-Atlantean culture; and my reason for doing so will emerge in the course of today's lecture.

Within this post-Atlantean cultural epoch that we're calling Central European, the most varied national elements have been conjoined for many centuries. And it is this conjoining of the various national elements that makes it impossible to speak of a "national" culture within Central Europe in the same way one has to speak of a national culture in the case of the southern and western peoples of Europe.

Of course when we consider this Central European culture we have to attend first of all to the fact that today it appears as a fusion of the peoples of two different state formations. Please note that in all of these discussions I intentionally speak of cultures rather than states.[95] So let me indicate here that Central European culture arises from a fusion of two different state formations: it's a fusion of the German Empire and Austria.

In the case of Austria, we see immediately that it would be downright absurd to speak of the nation-state, for Austria-Hungary is an amalgamation of many different national cultures. That was history's doing, as it were: Austrian life consists of the interplay of these national cultures. And in the same way history brought it about that the culture of the German Empire now appears within a unified structure.[96] But if we ask about the culture of the inhabitants of Germany, and about the culture of the German-speaking population in Austria (which is of course connected in many ways with the populace of Germany, even geographically, but on the other hand is separated from it geographically by imposing mountain ranges), then our first task is to inquire about something we could call the "German element."

Having identified this German element, now imagine posing the question: What is German? It's impossible to pose this question in the same way that we could ask: What is French?—What is English?—What is Italian?—with regard to each of those national cultures. We can't because the denizens of "German culture"—if we insist on using that expression—ultimately have no idea (in any particular epoch they have never had any idea) what criterion they want to use to define themselves.

If pressed, someone who answered "I am a German" would have to change what she meant by that after a relatively short time. She would have to modify the concept of "Germanness" continuously as she moved from one era to the next.

It's telling that during Germany's travails [in the Napoleonic wars] even Fichte[97] struggled to clarify the concept "German" in his famous *Addresses to the German Nation*.[98] In two of these addresses he grappled with the concept of "Germanness,"[99] and he struggled to come to terms with the concept "German" in the way one does regarding something objective. His relationship to the concept was not the usual subjective one that we see when people are struggling to come to terms with the concept of their nationality.

Within the striving of the denizens of Central Europe lies something we can only characterize as "a striving to *become* something" rather than "a striving to *be* something." To *become* something, not to *be* it. Hence within this Central Europe that I'm describing, anyone who is self-conscious would actually have to rebel against ever being classified according to any kind of concept. No, she wants first to become what she actually is; what she is to become hovers before her as a kind of ideal. And that's why the most authentic expression of the inmost striving of Central Europe is Goethe's *Faust*.[100] "'Whoever strives in ceaseless toil, / Him we may grant redemption',"[101] or "He only earns both freedom and existence / Who must reconquer them each day."[102] What we see is Becoming within Being; a Being that never stands still; a striving-toward-something;[103] toward what one actually wants to be, viewed from afar.[104]

Thus we can say: Out of the "fluid" striving of human nature there had to arise that work which is so characteristic of the nature of Central Europe: just this work on Faust by Goethe. For all its perfections Goethe's *Faust* displays countless imperfections; as a work of art, it's anything but complete and unified. This *Faust* could be rewritten in a later epoch; it could be written in a completely different way and yet it would still express the essence, this archetype, of Central European humanity. If you let this archetype impress itself upon you, then you'll gradually develop an imagination of the fundamental Central European disposition as the I striving ever higher, entwined by snakes. Entwined by snakes! That means striving within a still indeterminate wisdom, striving within a wisdom that is still forming itself,[105] striving within a wisdom *in statu nascendi*, fundamentally devoid of any kind of security, never feeling complete in one's inner being—that is the nature of Central European humanity. "And here, poor fool, I stand once more, / No wiser than I was before."[106]

And then Faust's ascension into the spiritual world at the end of Part Two. It might be said that Goethe turns Faust into a "messenger of the gods" here. Surely there's no better way to express this visually than by employing a caduceus.[107]

And there's yet another way in which this German element can best be characterized by saying that its members are messengers.[108] The archetypal spiritual emissary was Mercury.[109] You need only look at the accumulated evidence and you will find that the deeper task of the German-speaking world has been to serve as emissaries of culture.[110]

Let me point out some particulars; let's consider the culture of Austria in just this regard. If you study the Austrian state, this remarkable, complicated state formation, you come to know three splinter groups. You might say that for the most part they have now disappeared or are in the process of disappearing. These are the inhabitants of northern Hungary, the Carpathian or Slovak Germans; certain inhabitants of Transylvania; and certain inhabitants of the Lower Theiss region, the Banat.[111]

What kind of peoples were those? Those were all peoples from western regions who migrated in earlier centuries, peoples who brought along their German thoughts and language. One such splinter group settled south of the Carpathian Mountains in northern Hungary—in my youth people still called them the Carpathian Germans. Today, for the most part, they've been assimilated into Magyar culture. They've given up almost completely the substance of their own culture, but it lives on within the substance of Magyar culture. It hasn't disappeared; it lives on within a great number of impulses within Magyar culture, and also in the achievements of the industrious people of northern Hungary. They have not clamored to stand apart from the surrounding cultures; essentially they have not resisted the sacrifice of their "Germanness."

In Siebenbürgen you find the Siebenbürgen Saxons; they are of Rhenish descent. I got to know them personally in 1889 when I gave a lecture in Hermannstadt.[112] Today they are in the process of being assimilated into Magyar culture, just like the Carpathian Germans. The substance of their culture lives on, it has been absorbed into Central European culture, but the people of Siebenbürgen have made no claim to stress their own separate national element.

The peoples of the southern Theiss region, the so-called Banat, are real emigrated Swabians. They emigrated from the area around present-day Württemberg. Exactly the same thing happened to them as happened to the Carpathian Germans: they were the emissaries of something that has now been absorbed into another language, into a completely different national form—real emissaries. And the better you understand the real situation, the more you realize how necessary it was that these peoples be absorbed into a Central European element, so that this Central European element could flourish as such.

Countless similar cases could be adduced. Anyone who strives for real comprehension and is not satisfied to judge according to stereotypes will see in such matters vivid and concrete evidence of the overcoming of the national element, of a suppression of the principle of nationalism.[113] The fundamental tendency in Central Europe is one that lifts its inhabitants out of the principle of nationalism in order to realize "the human as such." Hence it would be foolish to call *Faust* "German," even though it could emerge only within Central Europe, even though it belongs among the works that are representative of Central Europe in the truest sense.

My dear friends, if you really want to understand such issues, then you have to take heed of the various intertwinings within the evolution of human culture. These various intertwinings show us for example—looking to the things I said yesterday—that a rebirth of Greek antiquity took place within French culture. Of course Greek antiquity lives in a certain sense within German art as well, especially in German literature, and someone could very well say: Hasn't the Greek Iphigenia been reborn in Goethe's drama?[114] Didn't Goethe write a drama about Achilles, or at least part of one?[115]

You really have to get to the bottom of these things in order to be able to see that of course ancient Greece revives within the whole of the fifth post-Atlantean epoch, but the important thing is that, in the same way that it lived within the larger culture of the intellectual or mind soul, it also lived within the corresponding elements of French culture, the elements of the intellectual or mind soul. It doesn't live within the mentality of the individual Frenchman, in his individuality, but rather in the folk-soul. It lives within the whole *way* of being[116] of this folk-soul. In the minds of individual Frenchmen it lived perhaps even less consciously than it did in Goethe or Schiller when they formed their views about the ways in which ancient Greece surfaced again within French culture. But in all the ways that the folk-soul influences culture, within this folk-soul of France, we find Greek antiquity rises up and lives again.

Of course we could refer to the things Voltaire wrote in a letter of 1768: "I have always believed, I still believe, and I shall always believe that, as far as tragedy and comedy are concerned, Athens has been surpassed by Paris in every regard ... I make bold to declare that all of the Greek tragedies look like school exercises when compared with Corneille's glorious scenes and the consummate art of Racine's tragedies."[117] And you could also compare that with Schiller's letter to Goethe where he says, in so many words: Because you were born neither as a Greek nor as an Italian; since you were born in this cold, Northern clime, you had to allow an ideal Greece to arise within yourself.[118] Nevertheless we have to admit that the form Ancient Greece assumed when it arose in Central Europe was inadequate compared to its reemergence within French culture. If you study [Goethe's drama] *Iphigenia*, what you find there is a longing for Ancient Greece. Goethe felt that he came to understand art differently after having experienced it in Italy—and yet, what lives in Goethe's *Iphigenia* is something completely different from what lives in a Greek work of art. There would be much to say about the ways in which such artistic works have taken shape, but in these lectures I can give only a hint of them.

The revival of the intellectual soul within the French folk-soul manifests itself in their whole way of life. When we see how Voltaire denigrates the whole of human history, he comes across to us as utterly Greek. Of course people have indulged in all kinds of fantastic notions about Greek antiquity. But if you know what Greek antiquity was and then you read a little poem by Voltaire, then you get a feeling of what I mean by the rebirth of Greek culture. Voltaire's little poem contains the following sentiment: "Full of beauties and errors, / Old Homer has my esteem; / Like all his heroes, he is / Garrulous, overdone, and yet sublime."[119]

No Greek could have spoken in this way about Homer, of course, but the Greeks spoke in this way about other things. This is a thoroughly Greek tone.

If we sought to characterize Central Europe succinctly, we would—even just as a matter of geographical necessity—substitute for the concept of nationalism "striving for individuality." And with this phrase "striving for individuality" we would be able to characterize not just Germans, but also a great number of other Central European cultures. They all exhibit this striving for individuality to the very highest degree. Despite all the superficial differences among these various peoples, we find it in the Czechs, in the Ruthenians,[120] in the Slovaks, in the Magyars, and finally we see it in that polar antithesis of German culture,[121] in the Poles. In the case of the Poles, everything is saturated with individualism to an extreme degree. Hence the intensely individualistic worldviews of the great Polish men Towianski, Slowacki, and Mickiewicz[122]—worldviews that flow from their individual personalities. It doesn't matter whether you like or dislike Polish philosophy; that's not what's important here. You have to look at these things objectively. When the Polish element of religion appears, we can always disregard the fact that the thinker in question is a Pole.[123]

And so that's how it is with this whole conglomeration of peoples[124] that makes up the culture of Central Europe: there is a striving for individuality that manifests as a common property.[125] Polish Messianism is just a different manifestation of this same striving for individuality; there you see it framed more abstractly, set forth more as a philosophical ideal. But it's the same thing that comes to expression in Goethe's *Faust* as personal striving, as the striving of an individual personality.

The right motif to express this individual element that comes into play within Central Europe is this caduceus [Fig. 6]. The element that descends from on high has two components, which are indicated by the binary motif above it. It has to take on a bifurcated form because it has to express, on the one hand, the idealism that's present in Central Europe and, on the other hand, things of a more practical nature. What matters here is not the relative sizes, but rather that one is next to the lower motif and the other arches over it.

Fig. 6

The forms that arch above the caduceus express the characteristically tenuous connection between the peoples of Central Europe and the soil upon which they stand, how that's more the case in one group and less in another. The caduceus itself represents Central Europe's element of thought, its inclination towards philosophical speculation. Even foreigners' jokes about Germans contain these two elements, albeit with little understanding of them. It's been said of Germans that they can cultivate the land and they can sail through the skies, but they'll never rule the seas.[126] (By "sail through the skies" they didn't mean hot air balloons, but rather German otherworldliness.[127]) It's a strange judgment if one thinks of the German Hanseatic League,[128] but that's the judgment that was made.

Here [in Fig. 6] we see dripping down from above these two innately German characteristics, which are also more broadly Central European characteristics.

The I represents the element in the human soul that must come to terms with itself above all. Hence we will find within this element of the I a great inner turmoil and ferment. Although the Germans have waged war outwardly, and will do so in the future, their most characteristic wars are those that Germans have fought against Germans so that the I would arise within. If you follow these latter wars, then you have a truer image of the wars that unfold within the human I itself.

I once pointed out that the human I would never be able to achieve full self-consciousness if it were not enkindled anew each morning by the external world. This thought is contained in many places in my lectures. The I enkindles self-consciousness through contact with the outer world. Otherwise the I would exist, but it would not become fully conscious. All of the guidance that anthroposophy provides regarding human nature is confirmed by the external facts.

In a sense, the external configuration exhibited by the nation-states of Central Europe did not originate from these states themselves. Rather, it was something determined from without. If I begin by speaking about Austria, then I have to say: In my youth there were many people in Austria who always used to say that Austria, this conglomeration of peoples, would simply have to dissolve very soon; there's no way it could hold together; it was ripe for dissolution. People who knew some history didn't believe it, because they knew that Austria was not just held together from within but also pushed together from without. That's something I could demonstrate historically, right down into the smallest details.

And if we were really objective about the latest configuration of the German Empire, then we would have to say: Of course the Germans have been talking forever about a single German Empire; it has long hovered before them as an ideal. But perhaps it would still not be there today if the French hadn't declared war in 1870 and thereby forced the unification of Germany. The founding of the German Empire actually was determined from outside in the same way that the I enkindles its consciousness every morning through the external world. Otherwise unification would probably remain only an envisioned goal, an ideal within the thoughts of the inhabitants.

All of these matters need to be weighed entirely objectively, especially by those who want to adhere rigorously to the principles of anthroposophy. That's the only way we can survey, calmly and dispassionately, what's unfolding within the fifth post-Atlantean epoch. All I can do today is provide a few scattered guidelines—even fifty lectures would not suffice to cover everything that I have to say on this subject! But every one of those fifty lectures would deliver new evidence of the truth of the few words that I'm able to offer here today.

That's the basis of our claim that anthroposophists can rise to an imagination of European culture that will serve as a prototype for the harmonious interaction of the sentient soul, the intellectual or mind soul, the consciousness soul and the I. And it can stand before our soul as a high ideal if we say to ourselves: The insights that anthroposophy has given us about the harmonious interaction of these individual faculties allow us to make our own contribution to the overcoming of the chaotic interactions we see unfolding before us. We can help to realize an ideal of harmonious interaction—an ideal for the inner lives of our individual souls as well.

But that will be possible only if each and every individual struggles to attain objectivity. *The individual human being stands higher than the nation!* At the present time this truth has been obscured on many sides. I'm simply compelled to make such observations. It's my spiritual duty to say these things to you, and it's only because it's my spiritual duty that I make these comments at the present time.

Today we live in a time in which our vision of the harmony among the faculties of the various folk-souls[129] appears to have been clouded more than ever. We have been blinded to everything that's unfolding all around us. I won't foreground what's happening on the battlefields; other necessities come into play there. Rather, I want to stress what's happening in the judgments that are being made about the various peoples. All of that seems to contradict what ought to be happening in the fifth post-Atlantean epoch.

As I've said in many previous lectures here, I felt that my own experience in writing my book *The Riddles of Philosophy* was symptomatic. The second volume of this book has just appeared. I had written the text through page 206 when the war broke out. Only what comes after page 206, "A Brief Outline of an Approach to Anthroposophy,"[130] was written during the war. In the second volume I had sought to characterize the philosophies of Bergson[131] and Boutroux[132] in an objective fashion. I believe that, in light of the small space available, anyone would consider my depiction objective. Of course I had to take note of the fact that Bergson's philosophy is not original, and that there is a sense in which it is flimsy. On pages 199 through 204, I present the philosophical positions of Boutreux and Bergson without making any judgments, and then I have written on page 204: "From lightly woven and easily attainable thoughts like this, Bergson produces an idea of evolution that had been expressed previously in a profound mode of thought by W. H. Preuss in his book, *Spirit and Matter* (1882)."[133] And then I cover the thoughts of the solitary thinker Preuss on pp. 205-206. Of course Bergson was obliged to know about Preuss's work. Let me repeat emphatically: Bergson was obliged to know about Preuss's work, because a philosopher must know the philosophy of his contemporaries if he wants to write. I ask you please to note that I say: He is obliged to know the things I indicated—I put it this way so that no one will claim I accused Bergson of intentionally hiding his debt to Preuss. I didn't say that.

Let's imagine everything that the various nations have said about each other, and everything that's happened over the past several weeks had not taken place. Then the words I wrote about Bergson would simply stand as an objective account. Needless to say, there's no context in which I would be able to express a different judgment regarding this fact [about Bergson]. Anyone who works on an anthroposophical basis has to remain objective. But the same fact comes up in a speech that was held on September 10, 1914. The speech bore the title "On the Real War," and it was given by a philosopher who is also known in France, Wilhelm Wundt.[134]

"It's not what you say, but how you say it."[135] I've seldom felt the wisdom of this old saw as strongly as when I read through this speech. For what is it that Wundt says about a remark that Bergson is supposed to have made? I have to believe that Bergson didn't really make the remark, because it's hard to imagine him saying anything so foolish.[136] So what is it that Wundt says? "What makes this war so difficult and painful for us is that it is at bottom a war against our own relatives. And however much the spiritual nature of the Britons may have changed since the days of Ancient Britain—in my opinion, not for the better—nevertheless more than any other country England is the spiritual brother of Germany. Compared with that, what do we care about the Belgians, who have started this war with their reckless shortsightedness in order to demonstrate to the world once and for all their utter inability to exist as a separate state? And who among us doesn't feel genuine sympathy for beautiful France, the vast majority of whose populace didn't want this war, but was dragged into it by the unconscionable ambition of a handful of adventuresome politicians? And we will withhold harsh judgment even of those bombastic journalists who want to settle the score regarding this self-imposed humiliation of France with foolish slanders of the German people. Why should it matter to us if Mr. Henri Bergson,[137] whom no reputable philosopher in Germany has ever taken seriously, calls us barbarians? For we know that this philosopher has stolen all his thoughts of any value from us barbarians so that he could dress them up afterward in his tawdry rhetoric and send them out into the world as his own discovery."

This is no way for the culture of the I to speak about the culture of the intellectual soul! Here Wundt has obscured precisely what needs to be seen clearly. But if a sufficient number of people have taken anthroposophy to heart; if they really have allowed themselves to be permeated by anthroposophy, then this eclipse will give way to the ideal that must emerge from us out of our working with the truths of anthroposophy. Only if we enter deeply enough into the truth of these matters will we gain the right sense for them. If you want to experience the truth of the various cultures' mutual relationships, you should read the signs representing the meanings embodied in our columns and architraves. You need to engage in a kind of palmistry,[138] accompanied by the right kinds of feelings. Contemplate the various convolutions of the formal motifs expressed there, and you will understand the various spiritual relationships among the several nations. There isn't one single motif that's a matter of chance. With every motif you should ask: What does it signify? When you look at this motif and see how it metamorphoses into that of the third column, then what you see expressed at the same time is the interaction between the cultures to which both columns refer. Out of these motifs of the columns and the architraves you can read the structural relationships among the inner lives of the various peoples.[139]

And if you go to Russian culture in the East,[140] there you will find what makes us fully human by taking up into our soul and harmonizing there everything that is good, everything excellent from all the various individual cultures. We hope that this will resound like a symphony in the second, smaller structure, underneath the smaller cupola of our building. When we proceed further eastward this motif is conjoined to another [Fig. 7]:

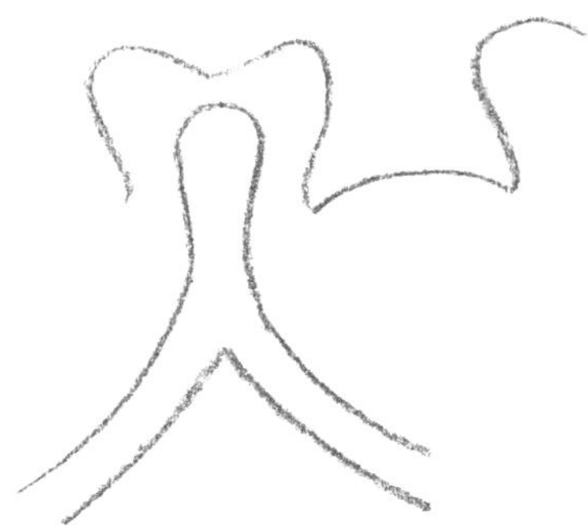

FIG. 7

We see how this figure is a metamorphosis of the caduceus. But we also see that whereas the caduceus spreads out its serpentine motif horizontally within the world, here the central motif culminates above, and forks out below in order to receive, in order to take up what comes from above like a blossom opening itself from above downwards.

This is a Jupiter motif. (The caduceus is a Mercury motif.) It expresses the Jupiter culture of the European East. It expresses this culture through the "serpentness"[141] of the motif, which is directed entirely upward, and also in the "foldedness,"[142] which reaches out like folded hands towards that which comes down from above. Past it glides something that opens downward from above like a blossom, and with which the earthly human being must connect.

This motif—and thus what underlies it—is difficult for Europeans to grasp because it is connected to the future, because it is more of the future than the present. Because of the fundamental nature of contemporary language, it is extraordinarily difficult even to find the words to express what is hiding behind this motif. It's so extraordinarily difficult because, the moment we arrive at this motif, the words immediately need to mean something completely different from what they meant previously if we want to capture the nature of the matter adequately. We can't speak of a "Russian" nature in the same sense that we can speak of "English," "French," or "Italian" characteristics. We have already seen that in the case of Central Europe it isn't possible to speak of a national culture in the same way we can of Western European nations. Even less can we talk about Russia as a nation in the same way we can with Western European peoples. For if we look toward Russia, do we see something like what we see when we look to the English, French, and Italian peoples? No! There's something in Russian culture that is a complete transformation of Western European culture.

In the West, we see national cultures, and we can find our way into their natures by immersing ourselves in the cultural phenomena they produce. In trying to understand what it means to be German, we find a striving, something unfinished,[143] a striving for something that has not yet arrived, something that exists only as an ideal. But this striving lives within the blood, within the astral and the etheric body of the Central European. If we look to the East, we see a monumental, coherent culture uniting religion and philosophy, a culture that is eminently religious. But should we call it Russian? It would be absurd to call it Russian—even if the Russians themselves do so—because it's actually a continuation of the ancient Byzantine culture.

It's entirely natural that the contents of the sentient soul originate within the sentient soul, and that what lives within the intellectual or mind soul stems from the intellectual or mind soul, and the content of the consciousness soul from the consciousness soul. And it's natural that the contents of the I, even though it's inherently fluid and ever-becoming, flows from the I. But that which descends from the spirit self[144] is something that precipitates out of the spirit within the other faculties of sentient soul, the intellectual or mind soul, and the consciousness soul.

We know that we must construe the human soul as composed of sentient soul, intellectual or mind soul, consciousness soul, and I. And then the spirit self inclines from above, down into these other four bodies. The spirit self announces its advent as something alien that comes over the national identity, as though trickling down from above.

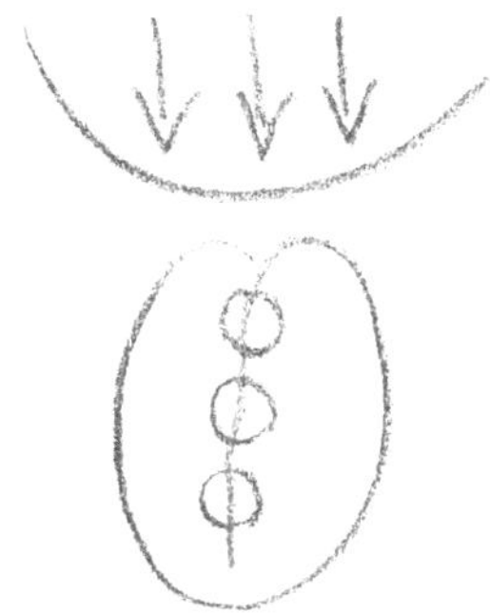

FIG. 8

And so we see that essentially everything Russia has experienced heretofore as its culture is alien to it—alien from the moment in which a Greek-Byzantine culture was sought, right up to the institutions that were brought in from the outside by Peter the Great.[145] And so we see that the spirit self is the conduit through which the forces flow down to the faculties of the soul, and that the spirit self will receive its true force and its true nature only in the future. The Russian soul must begin preparing to receive, and becoming accustomed to receiving, this spirit self.

Needless to say, the foreign elements that have arrived within the Russian soul from without are not the spirit self of the future. But just as Byzantine Christianity, Eastern Orthodox religion, and Western culture have descended into the Russian soul, someday the spirit self will also descend. What we see today is only the preparation, the disposition to receive the spirit self.

Examples can be cited for each of these trends indicated by anthroposophy. Here is one that lies close to hand, and to which I have often referred. I have often emphasized the greatness of the philosopher Solovyov.[146] I first realized his greatness through clairvoyant research, which reveals that he has become even greater since his death in 1900. Since 1900 he has been able to accomplish even greater things than he was able to accomplish earlier.

But now let's look at the actual relationships. You can become convinced of this yourself by studying Solovyov's writings, many of which have been translated. We have the translations by Nina Hoffmann, by Ernst Keuchel, and then the excellent book that Frau von Vacano has translated, *The Spiritual Foundations of Life*.[147]

Now immerse yourself as a Central European in the works of Solovyov. You will have a remarkable realization, especially since the last of the aforementioned translations has become available. It really is extraordinarily interesting. Anyone who is equipped with everything that the philosophy of Western and Central Europe has to offer, and especially anyone who is a trained anthroposophist will ask of Solovyov: Well, what do you have to offer that is new vis-à-vis Central and Western European philosophy? Investigate what Solovyov has provided in comparison with Western thought. You won't find a single new idea! Everything you find is Western philosophy, word for word. Nothing is there, not even a turn of phrase, not the style nor the vocabulary—nothing that couldn't have been written equally well in the West!

And yet it *is* something completely different. But if you were to seek that difference in the philosophy, in what is said expressly so that it can be read like a usual Western European book, you would not find the otherness in that way. The otherness is not in the book itself, nor in any turn of phrase. It's not in the book itself, and yet it's contained there nevertheless. Truly, that otherness can be uncovered by a soul with the right sensibilities,[148] even while remaining convinced intellectually that the book contains nothing but Western philosophy.

The book contains a certain nuance of feeling that a Central European can experience like a very sultry atmosphere. You might say that it feels sometimes as though you were in an oven, especially when big, important questions are raised. But then, where such questions have been raised, you notice that nothing comes out in the way, in the style in which something comes out when reading the Western European philosophers. In place of that, a tone of feeling is struck that resonates like something infinite, like something expectant. It's a tone of feeling that has a mystical quality—to be sure, it's quite a sultry mysticism that can even be somewhat dangerous for any Central European who might enter into it.

Now if you're familiar with the human subconscious—and you really need to have gained such knowledge before entering into this peculiarly sultry mysticism—then this sultriness is certainly without danger. But anyone who is not acquainted with these deeper resonances[149] of the human soul can mistake this for Western philosophy and not realize the important differences. It's a peculiar phenomenon, a phenomenon that really goes to show how what comes from the East has not been spoken yet, has not been poured into words at all yet.

And we can come to know the peculiarities of the various European cultures if we call up the following before our souls. See for example how the whole French culture of the intellectual or mind soul is revealed in a single *mot* by Voltaire.[150] Anyone who has developed a sense for reading realities out of symptoms can't fail to see this. The witticism "If God did not exist, then He would have to be invented" has been ascribed to Voltaire, and rightly so. What that presupposes (for otherwise the phrase would be meaningless) is that one must believe in Him, for surely nobody would invent God for fun.

Only someone working entirely out of the intellectual or mind soul could have said such a thing—only someone who trusted the intellectual or mind soul completely, because invention is something that belongs to the intellectual soul.

Now let's take a Russian. Consider Bakunin.[151] He recast Voltaire's witticism, and the result is quite remarkable. He says, "If God existed, then it would be necessary to abolish Him!"[152] He says something along those lines.[153] Bakunin feels that if his own soul is to gain full validity, he cannot bear the thought that God exists. And another saying of Bakunin's[154] is very characteristic: "If God exists, then humans are slaves." That's one version; another runs: "Human beings are free—hence there is no God." And what Bakunin himself understands least is how we might escape this vicious circle. He says to himself: Now we want to choose. And he chooses the latter: "Human beings are free—hence there is no God."

I would say that Western European culture stands as the complete antithesis of the East on this issue. Up until now Western European culture had been able to unite the idea of the free human being with the idea of God, but Eastern European culture finds: If I am to be free—that is, if I am to think for myself—then no God may exist who compels me. Otherwise I am a slave. Nobody stands above me.

Here we feel the great chasm that stands between the sentient soul, intellectual or mind soul, consciousness soul, and I on the one hand, and the spirit self on the other, which still stands in the East as though in opposition to the West, preparing the advent of its own nature.[155] We feel the great chasm between the West and what we encounter coming out of the East. We feel the extent to which the East is unrelated to the West—we feel this in entirely characteristic ways when we see how representative figures from the East react to Western European culture. Who in the West can begin to understand what the Devil says to Ivan Karamazov,[156] unless she is already a student of Eastern culture? Who in the West understands immediately what Gorky[157] calls "a horrifying, but true truth"?[158]

"Yes, and what is truth? Human beings are the truth! What does it mean to be 'human' anyway? It's not you, and it's not me, and it's not them ... No! Rather, you, me, them, old Luka, Napoleon, Mohammed ... it's all of them together! That's it—something very great indeed! It's something that contains all beginnings and all endings ... Everything *within* human beings, everything *for* human beings. Only human beings exist, everything else—that's the work of their hands and of their brains! Human beings! Simply magnificent! It sounds so sublime: "h-u-u-u-man"! People should respect human beings! Not pity ... we shouldn't denigrate humanity through pity ... we should respect it!"[159]

And Gorky, a former actor—look how he talks about his relationship to the public! Listen to the former convict speaking! "I have always felt contempt for people who care too much about being well fed. That's not what life is about. Human beings are what matter! Humanity stands higher than a full stomach!"

It's very difficult to understand such things in the West, because they express the mystical suffering of the East. They point to the chasm that exists between what must come in Eastern Europe and what already exists in Western and Central Europe.

This immense chasm shows us that everything living in the East today is still not the East at all. I really would need to speak at length about this, but I can only allude to it. The East is something that still lives unspoken; it is something about which the East itself still knows little. The East is only beginning to sense and feel what it shall become in the future.

It will be very hard for the East, we understand that. It'll be very difficult for them to find a bridge to their own inner nature. It will be difficult for them to find themselves, because the phenomenon that confronts us here is no less than this: the East still lives within feeling, still lives within the ineffable. It's still seeking a form of expression; it's seeking it in the East, and it's seeking it in the West. In the East much still remains in the way of imported Byzantine influences: when the East speaks in this way, that's no longer its own inner nature speaking. A stranger is speaking, not the East itself.

But, my dear friends, there's one thing that *is* able to bridge these chasms: what we know as the true science of the spirit can bridge it. We've seen already that the evolution of Western and Central Europe can lead only to ultimate absurdity without anthroposophy.[160] And now we see that there simply isn't any possibility for progress in the relationship between Central and Eastern Europe, that it must succumb to madness, that there just isn't any way forward without the mutual understanding provided by anthroposophy. People will find and understand one another through anthroposophy. And they'll understand each other in such a way that not only their theoretical needs are met: through anthroposophy, the sufferings of whole cultures will be healed.

More than anywhere else, in the East we will have the opportunity to experience contemporary events as a powerful trial, for all the things that the East must eventually come to feel will stand in total opposition to the forces in the East that wanted this war. And even more so than in the West and even more so than in Central Europe, identification with the motives for war, the active motives that led to war, was a denial of the East's true nature. Therefore all the forces that led to this war must disappear in the East if redemption—if the sun of redemption is to rise over the East.

My dear friends, we really should take our building into our very hearts, because it expresses all this more profoundly than I can attempt to do by interpreting it with a few cursory words. You can feel what I just said much more profoundly when you see the building rightly, when you feel: "It contains everything." You only need to feel each convolution, and that protective power[161] living in those convolutions [of the motif in the architrave], really feel it. For our building should be one that people will call "a dome of mutual understanding for all Europeans." And in this way our building is perhaps, in a very special sense, an example of the dynamic I described in the Preface to my book *Theosophy*, where I wrote that anthroposophy is something that our age rejects with its intellect while longing for it with its soul. It's something that souls are actually demanding and need. They truly need it.

If we contemplate current events, then we can say that over the past several weeks anthroposophy has become utterly remote from the Europeans just when they should stand as close as possible to it, when they should desire it with every fiber of their hearts in their unconscious.[162] For when anthroposophy has really entered deeply into our hearts, in a way we can only hint at in these interpretations of the motifs of the columns and architraves, then the souls of the Europeans will come to stand in the right relationship to each other. And there's something even more important for the immediate present: if anthroposophy performs the task of really clarifying human thinking; if it really suffuses our thinking with clarity and straightens it out, then something of immense value will have been gained for the immediate future. For it's not just hearts that have become misaligned in our materialistic age, whose karma we are experiencing—our thoughts are also misaligned. People don't want mutual understanding. And worse—there may never have been a time in which there was such colossal lying on all sides as we have seen in our day. That's something, my dear friends, which is even worse than what's happening out there on the battlefields, because its effects last longer, because it works its way up into the spiritual world itself.

Actually it's slovenly thinking that has become our greatest talent! That's why I have to say: Anthroposophy is what humanity needs most urgently today.

Two questions present themselves: "Can people still think at all?"

and "Do people still feel that they must be in possession of the facts, the real truth of the matter at hand, before they think and speak about it?"

For the reasons I just gave, the spiritual world has obligated me to pose these questions.

The former president of the United States, Theodore Roosevelt, has called what lives in Central Europe "Bernhardism." I don't want to speak about what this former president said. All I want to do is give you just a taste of the kinds of things that usually go unnoticed. He's referring to Bernhardi's book *Germany and the Next War*.[163] This book, which I'm holding here in my hand, needs to be taken very seriously, because the author knew a great deal about this war in an external way. That's why this book is so extraordinarily instructive from an exoteric perspective. But what is the real quality of the thinking behind such an outwardly respectable book?

In the book there is a chapter entitled "The Right to Declare War." Of course, in asserting a "right to declare war," one must take the position that nations are to be valued more highly than human beings as individuals—one must speak out of the consciousness of Luciferic and Ahrimanic beings.[164] In this chapter there is a sentence that the author meant in the best way possible given his point of view. He tries to explain why it is that, as long as there are nations, those nations will have the right to wage war upon each other. The sentence reads: "Just as morally there is nothing greater an individual can do than sacrifice his life for his conviction, than give his own life for the cause that it serves; or even for the bare concept of the value of the ideals possessed by a moral individual...." Very nice, he characterizes the highest degree of autonomy as an ideal. And then he continues: "... In the same way, there's nothing more sublime that nations and states can do than devote their last ounce of energy to their own self-assertion, their own honor and dignity."

Well, my dear friends, it's hard to imagine a more beautiful *salto mortale*![165] For the first half of the sentence states something that's true enough in isolation, but taken together with the conclusion in the back half of the sentence, it's the craziest thought imaginable. States can't adopt a selfless standpoint. That's a completely different situation. It's important for us to gain clarity about that. For example, put yourself in the shoes of an Austrian statesman after all the events that led up to the assassination by a Serb in Sarajevo.[166] Does it make any sense to speak in a way that Bernhardi describes? Absolutely not! The statesman has to act according to the egoism that the state imposes upon him. That's only one example of the way in which things are said today out of a thinking that's completely false. Here's a place where anthroposophical perspectives are eminently suited to provide clarity, if only there are enough people able to engage in it. These are not just little details; such things are a big deal.[167] For it's just such moments that have come together and led today to the horrific outbreak of war. I really believe I know what I'm saying here. I'm telling you this because at the same time I really can say—if you'll allow me to speak as an esoteric teacher—because I really have suffered enough in light of the events of the last several weeks, and I'm still suffering enough, and I've had enough shattering experiences, beginning with the assassination at Sarajevo and many other things besides. I myself have never seen, nor have I heard an esoteric teacher describe anything like the astonishing events that followed the assassination in Sarajevo. A soul[168] was raised up into the spiritual world in such a way that it began behaving unlike any other soul, becoming something like a cosmic soul, forming something like a cosmic power nexus[169] around which every conceivable element of fear gathered itself. Every element of fear that was there raced over to that soul. And now, in the spiritual world everything has the opposite effect: in the physical world, fear held back the war, but in the spiritual world it was an element promoting war; it led with rapid steps to war.

Experiencing for the first time what I just described is one of the most shattering esoteric observations anyone can make. Someday, when people look back objectively upon the events of the past eight to ten weeks, just by following those outer events, they will begin to recognize something that is a mirror image of the spiritual world.[170]

More than ever, our task as anthroposophists today is to learn objectivity; it's to learn genuine objectivity from the events going on around us. We are very, very far from having achieved this objectivity today. And I sought to come to terms with this issue by asking two questions. The first—"Can people still think?"—I tried to answer rather negatively, shall we say. The other question was: "Do people seek the facts when they want to think or speak today? Is that what people do?"

Everywhere we look, we see such colossal lying on all sides! Whole nations are lying to each other on a colossal scale. Nobody feels any obligation to serve the truth first and foremost, to get to the bottom of the real facts.

The duty to examine the facts must be taken to heart by anthroposophists as something of immense and profound importance. We have to learn that important people simply cannot be saying the kinds of things that are being said on all sides.

Endless examples could be adduced, of course. Let me give just one example; many, many others could be given.

I have a letter here before me, both the original English and a translation into German. It's a letter that a number of theologians wrote to Professor Harnack in Berlin.[171] I didn't take this letter from the newspaper, because that's the last place to look for the truth these days. If you want to know the truth, you have to look past the accounts in the press. This letter begins: "Honored Sir: We, the undersigned, a group of theologians who owe more than we can express to you personally and to the great host of German teachers and leaders of thought, have noticed with pain a report of a speech recently delivered by you, in which you are said to have described the conduct of Great Britain in the present war as that of a traitor to civilization."

Anyone who wants to form a judgment regarding this open letter has to do more than simply read it: she has to decide whether the first sentence is true. It's *not* true! For if you actually read what Harnack said, you'll find that he said nothing about wanting to accuse Great Britain of having betrayed civilization. It's much ado about nothing. Harnack's rhetoric may have been gratuitous and hollow,[172] but that's another matter. Now imagine that someone who doesn't know what Harnack actually said should read the letter written by the English theologians. What would someone think? The open letter has been printed and reprinted in various places. Poisonous lies have been spread by people who enjoy the world's respect, and believe that they have a strong moral conscience.

I wanted to mention only this minor episode, which is terrible enough, because as anthroposophists we have to feel keenly the need to see such things clearly. Otherwise, there's no way out of the cultural chaos in which we find ourselves. We have to hew strictly and earnestly to our fundamental principle: "Only in the truth can we find real wisdom."[173] Our whole building is an embodiment[174] of this principle. Everything depends on being able to read its forms. If you read them correctly, then your heart will feel the earnestness, the conscientiousness, the yearning for truth with which they confront everything that is present in cultural and spiritual life today.

If all our friends would constantly bear in mind that the truth is founded on facts, then their work will be much more salutary, everywhere, regardless of their nationality. But if they take their stand on the basis of a one-sided conception of nationality, then they never will be able to accomplish what anthroposophy is calling upon them to do.

What made Blavatsky's Theosophy impossible is that, right from the beginning, the interests of one part of humanity—not those of the English, but of Indians!—were placed above the interests of humanity as a whole. And it's profoundly true that we arrive at esoteric truths only by serving the interests of humanity as a whole rather than those of any particular group. We have to do it earnestly, with real, profound, earnest feeling. Esoteric truths go dark the moment we put the interests of any particular group ahead of the interests of humanity as a whole. Difficult as that task may be in a time like this, anyone who wants to call him- or herself an "anthroposophist" in the true sense of the word must strive to attain that ideal.

Lecture 4

Dornach, October 24, 1914

Last time, and the time before that, we sought to interpret the forms of our building's columns. Many different interpretations are possible, but we have sought one that flows quite naturally from the forms themselves.

Entering the building from the west, it's possible to feel united with all of humanity. The motifs of the capitals express the forces at work in the various cultures, whereas the architraves express the relationships among them.

It will perhaps have occurred to one or another of you that I haven't referred to all of the European—what shall we call them?—peoples or cultural communities. It's just not always possible to include everything on every occasion, because the point is not to make dogmatic indications, but rather to represent the principles involved. In connection with the motifs of the capitals that we have discussed, I've described innate tendencies or impulses within the souls of specific European cultures. I've described the souls of the Italian and Spanish cultures, or rather those that inhabit the southern and southwestern peninsulas; and I've described tendencies that are innate within the peoples who dwell in Western Europe, Central Europe, and in Eastern Europe. I proceeded in the way that I did because I wanted initially to choose those cultural communities which exhibit qualities that can be expressed by a motif, where the motif of the capital expresses what lives within the cultural community. Hence a relationship exists between motif and cultural community.

And indeed, moving from west to east, the second column represents the cultural communities of the Italian and the Iberian peninsulas. The third column represents French culture; the fourth, British culture, and so on.

Of course there are also other peoples within Europe. But I can't take up everything; instead, I'll have to restrict myself to speaking about the main principles. We might say that the cultures I described initially are the simpler cultures, however strange that might sound—simpler from an esoteric perspective at least.

From an esoteric perspective, cultures that are much more complicated than those already described would be for example Danish or Swedish or also Norwegian culture—for many things appear more complicated to the spiritual researcher even though they might appear much simpler to an observer upon the physical plane. Hence when we speak of Danish culture for example, the question can arise: What is the relationship to our motifs in that case? In that case, approaching the columns from the West, we would need to cast our gaze first upon the capital of the third column and then simultaneously upon the capital of the fifth column. We would need to contemplate the third *through* the fifth, as it were. You see, here it gets complicated, because we need to take two different capitals into account.

If we moved on to Sweden, then we'd have to take the second column and view it *through* the capital of the fifth.

If we proceeded to Norway, then we'd have to take the fourth column and view it *through* the capital of the fifth.

We would need to superimpose these capitals, so to speak. Then in the sensibility that arose through such superimposition we would begin to feel the expression of Danish, Swedish, and Norwegian culture in the same way that we gained such feelings for Italian-Spanish, French, British, and Central European culture by contemplating individual capitals.

It's really all here within the motifs of these capitals. And indeed it might gladden many hearts to study how things stand with Dutch culture, with Swiss culture, and so forth in light of the principle I've just set forth. I leave that to your own esoteric research.

So you see, when we speak about our building, truly there is nothing arbitrary here. None of these artistic forms allow the viewer simply to stand there and gaze upon them in the way that many of the formal motifs in contemporary paintings or other works of art compel us to look. Everything that we have assimilated from anthroposophy over the years is expressed in a way that's not merely theoretical or intellectual, but rather sensed and felt directly.[175] That's why it actually would be possible to talk about this building forever. But I leave it to you to flesh out and take to heart the various indications that I give. For it is the task of the building to bring hearts and souls into movement when they confront its motifs and formal relationships. It calls on us to interpret these matters not in some intellectual, allegorical way[176] but rather by allowing our hearts and minds and souls to speak when they find themselves within the space of the building and in the environs of the building.

We can begin to gain clarity about some things I want to bring to you today by considering a specific motif, namely four columns crowned by a cupola. We need to view such forms in an open-ended way; don't look upon it as though it stood in isolation. Nothing in the world remains closed within itself—no flower, no animal, no human being, and no such motif.

FIG. 9

For it's essential to realize that in the case of such a motif, forces are present that are quite separate from the form's geometrical context. In purely geometrical terms, this is four columns covered by a cupola. But the geometrical aspect is only one part of the motif. What is integral to the motif is a nexus[177] of forces that's latent within the universe as a whole, and makes it possible for the columns to bear the load of the cupola. The cupola rests upon the columns; the columns stand upon the earth: hence gravity comes into play.

In the case of such a motif, we must feel not just the geometry, but also the other elements that I have often called the dynamic or the forcely element.[178] We need to gain a feeling for the way in which things are situated within the nexus of dynamic forces at play within the whole universe, and especially the Earth.

If you contemplate this motif, you'll note that its characteristic quality is its symmetry when viewed from all sides. From every side, in every spatial direction—with regard to the cupola itself, of course—it is symmetrical, so that we can say: atop the earthly body a motif has been placed, which expands predominantly upward and is symmetrical around its circumference.

The important thing is to feel such a motif; we have to approach the motifs with an artistic sensibility. If we attempt to bring the right kind of sensibility to such a motif—and here of course it is a matter of really penetrating right down into the qualities of the forms, right down into what the form wants to express—then we will arrive at a point where we can say that this motif, which raises itself up above the earth and, at least in its upper portion, is symmetrical in every spatial direction, affects us in the same way as introspecting and experiencing our faculty of feeling inwardly.

You see, if you want to progress in esoteric studies, you must leave behind the one-sidedness of a purely abstract, intellectual point of view. Instead you have to adopt a way of looking that is founded upon experience. And so it is that I'm often compelled to speak experientially, and to avoid merely intellectual forms.

For most people today it's much more difficult to experience forms than it is to intellectualize about them. Here's an example of an experience: right at this moment I can only describe it as a thought experiment, but anyone who attempts to recapitulate what I say within their own experience can understand. How can we develop a sensibility for such a form and feel what it expresses? We can do it in the following way. When we wake up in the morning and get up out of bed to get on with our daily labors, we can raise into consciousness the thought: You just transitioned from a prone position—or, as many put it, lying down—to the activities of standing and walking. That's an experience. Admittedly an experience that few people raise up into consciousness, but the transition from a prone position into one of standing or walking is an experience. It is an experience. The experience that we are having is that when we are lying down gravity affects us like a sack, let's say a sack of flour. And what really affects us is gravity in a deeper sense, for whenever you're lying down, you're always lying on some surface of your body, and the surface exerts pressure upon the inner structure of your body, so that you are always pressing on the surface upon which you are lying. To be sure, usually you don't sense this pressure; but it is there; it's an impulse that's connected with the whole sensation of gravity, an impulse that works inward, as it were, into your astral body. What exists in the form of the surface under pressure works its way into your astral body.

Now when we begin to perceive what affects us as a pressured surface, we simultaneously perceive the elementary spirits of the earth.[179] That's just the place in which we can perceive them well, because when we stand and walk we're able to perceive them only by means of the pressure that's exerted through the soles of the feet.

Now, when you stand up, you leave the sphere of this pressure. You set yourself up in opposition to gravity. You situate the axis of your own body within the field of gravity. You no longer give yourself over to gravity like a sack—you enter actively into the sphere of gravity. That is an experience, an experience that we certainly have in a way that's different from any experience of thought by the brain thinking in abstractions.

In the lectures I gave on *Inner Reading and Inner Hearing*,[180] I said that there are actually three brains. Once we begin to make use of it, the middle brain experiences things in a thoroughly vital way; we begin to have an experience of feeling, as it were, within the midbrain.

So, we have stood up and become conscious of the experience of standing up; then we have the experience of feeling our way into the world.[181] Only then do we begin to know what feeling really is. There are many other ways to do this, but we begin to know a bit what feeling really is when we have the experience of standing up in this way.

So you have to start by making this experience of standing up really conscious. Then you can have an experience of these forms [in Fig. 9] by saying to yourself: This form differentiates itself from me because it can't stand up—it always stays lying down. If it wanted to attain my level of experience, it would have to stand up; it would have to rotate itself ninety degrees and form a perpendicular. What this cupola has heavenward,[182] by striving upwards with the form of its dome, is something that we human beings have when we have stood up. We have it especially when we feel our way around in the world[183] using our hands. If we as human beings could experience what's above us while lying down, we would feel with our hands above us something of the nature of a dome. In the sphere of feeling lies hidden what's expressed within such an architectural motif. In the feelsphere.[184]

If it were possible for us as human beings to be fastened to the earth somehow in a prone position, and to feel our way spiritually with our hands, to grope our way out into the world,[185] then we would feel our way into the spiritual world above ourselves as though we were within a mighty dome, a structure that's symmetrical in all dimensions.

Fig. 10

The Greeks experienced something like this. Hence we feel an apparent contradiction within one aspect of Greek culture, given that it arose predominantly out of the intellectual or mind soul. There's an apparent contradiction, but we have to get used to such contradictions when we begin to study things esoterically. Greek culture arose within a placid union of humanity with the earth. The Greeks felt united with the earth by having developed a placid relationship, by having felt their way into the heavens above them as into a spiritual dome.

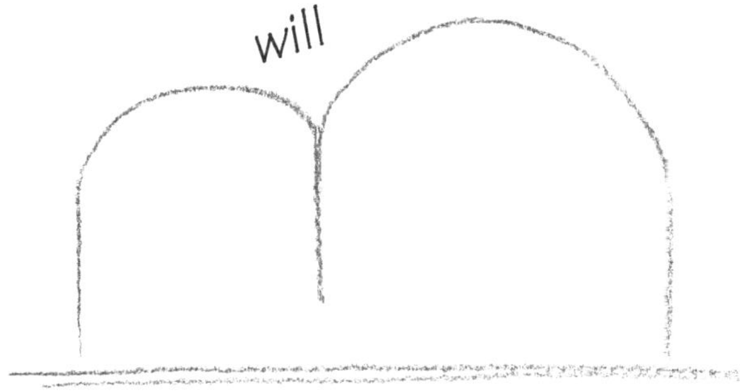

FIG. 11

Living today, we don't feel the same inner promptings as the Greeks; the fundamental tone of our inner life is different. And that's especially true of the new developments within human evolution that are only just beginning to express themselves in our building. What has to happen now is that, arising after its rest, humanity must not only stand up but really begin to walk. In addition to the sphere of feeling, we have to get to know the sphere of will artistically. The only way to accomplish that is by transforming symmetry *in all dimensions* into the kind of symmetry that has only *one* axis. And so it's possible to say: The moment we transform the architectural motif so that it has only *one single* axis of symmetry, then what we have expressed in the building is not just the experience of a human being transitioning from rest into feeling. We've also expressed a humanity that's transitioning from feeling into will, into walking. A motif of forward movement is the motif of the will.

That's why when anyone enters the building they will begin to have an inner experience: in contemplating the motifs of the separate capitals and architraves, she will feel she is being "pushed forward"; she will feel she is moving forward. This is something that is expressed in the ways I have indicated already in the two previous lectures.

Now the human will is the faculty that's most closely connected with unconscious experiences. We might say that for us moderns it's the place where we're guided most by the gods. The will is the place where the gods are most at work guiding us, and it goes without saying that Lucifer and Ahriman are also at work there. That's why there is such a thing as an evil will. But the will is borne by the gods, impelled forward, and it's only in the rarest cases that we're in a position to know what's occurring within our wills. That's why the things that we express involuntarily when we speak, the things of which we're least conscious, are those toward which our will is disposed, and those that are caused by our will. And we can even say in that regard: Rightly so.

Initially we don't have the slightest need to be fully conscious when we surrender to the primal, elementary nature of our will, when we allow the impulses of the gods to act within our will. The most elemental impulses are the impulses of the will. And so we can progress in our incarnations from culture to culture—something that's represented in our building by the forward movement of the succession of columns.

We can progress from culture to culture; in each incarnation we're born into a different culture. What we experience out of our sphere of will proceeds in a sense from the gods. Initially there's little we can do to change this sphere of will. Someone who's born at a particular place on earth can't do anything to change the fact that she is born at a place represented by one or another motif in our columns. A person stands at this particular spot within evolution by dint of the unconscious depths of his or her will life.

This is what we have to imagine: that what comes to expression in this way rises up out of unconscious depths of the will. For example, the ways in which the inhabitants of the various nations think about each other, the way in which they—what shall we say—"praise" each other, is deeply connected with something that rises up like smoke as it were out of the depths of the will. All of that arises out of nothing other than impulses of the will.

The trajectory of human evolution reveals that it is possible for us to raise ourselves up out of blind impulses of will. But then we have to follow the corresponding movement in the other direction.[186] The direction of will-impulses is this one [leftward pointing arrow in Fig. 12], the direction of progress.[187] The direction of feeling-impulses however runs from below upward. As human beings we are capable of rising up above blind impulses of will. And it's by contemplating the motifs of the columns and architraves along the lines previously indicated that we're able to do this.

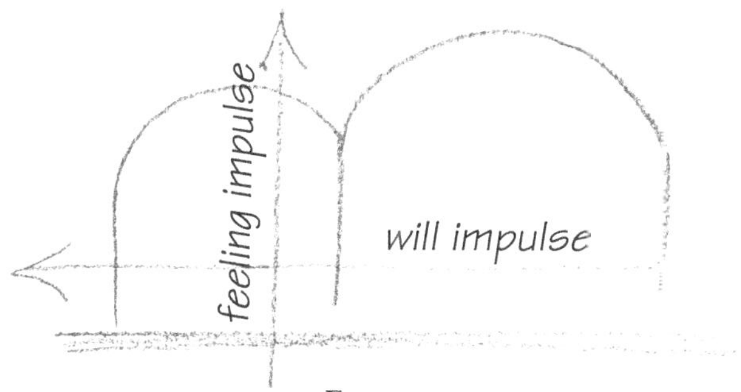

FIG. 12

Doesn't this kind of contemplation lift us up and allow us to see something in which we otherwise stand unconsciously? And isn't anthroposophy a means of achieving such a contemplative overview? Just think how much, infinitely much, humanity would benefit if the peoples of all cultures would understand each other, embrace each other lovingly, if all the things we discussed last time were taken up into a living feeling and a living knowing! How could a member of one cultural community simply hate and rail against a member of a different cultural community if she knew all the things we discussed last time?

How different the situation becomes when we know what evolution has apportioned to each of the several cultures! Then the constriction of the will that arises out of the realm of the will[188] is expanded into a harmony of all cultures.

We come to feel the several cultures as our own faculties within the inner life of our own souls. That's why we needed to express it in the vertical dimension of our building! It's actually the same thing to which the first article of our movement[189] refers as a theoretical, ethical principle. That same principle has actually been expressed concretely and in detail in the artistic forms of our building; you'll see the expression of it if you contemplate these forms as they rise from below upward. You'll see them in our building, and you'll experience them through our building.[190]

But of course the whole is always contained in each part. Thus we have more than just the direction of will-impulses [arrow pointing left, Fig. 12] and the direction of feeling-impulses [arrow pointing upward]. We have something further. We have something further because we can't just keep going upward arbitrarily: up above there's closure.

In speaking to you about this motif within our building, I've characterized it as something that bears weight and is oriented upward. But I can also characterize it as something that's achieving closure above, something that's covering, something that's covering over.[191] So in describing the motifs as a whole we might characterize them as progressing, lifting themselves up, closing themselves off.

You can also imagine a caduceus. If you bear it forwards, it's progressive; if you lift it up, then it raises itself up; if you compress the spiral at the top, letting it become inwardly rigid, then you experience a closing-off above. This closure at the top depicts the sphere of thoughts, in the same way that moving forward depicts the sphere of the will and moving upward depicts the sphere of feeling.

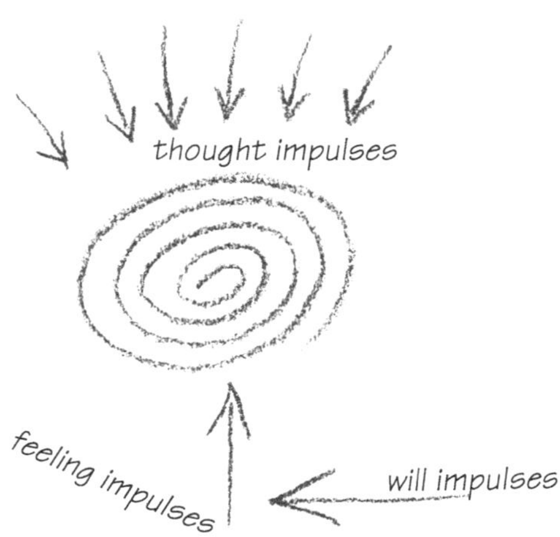

Fig. 13

People will gain a healthy feeling for human evolution by studying the motifs of our capitals and architraves, especially the way they raise themselves up from below. We could say that this is the basis for a mutual understanding of all the various cultures on earth.

If we want to rise up out of will into the sphere of feeling, then we have to overcome isolation by rising up, by actually participating in[192] this going-upward-from-below.[193] This movement will impart to the feelings, to the sympathies and antipathies of the inhabitants of the various cultural spheres, a certain something[194] that will become more and more necessary as the modern evolution of culture progresses.

We have to focus more upon the unconscious than upon what is present to immediate consciousness. The impulses of the will are part of the unconscious. More conscious than the impulses of will, yet still partially unconscious, are the impulses of feeling. Most conscious are the impulses of thinking, because whatever we might think, we're conscious of it—well, we're conscious of it, but only if we really think, if we really *live* in the thoughts. But we don't always live within the thoughts. When we speak, we allow the impulses of feeling and will to express themselves; often we speak right out of the realm of will or a feeling.

The peculiar thing about human nature is that when we speak, it's not always our thoughts that are expressing themselves. What passes for thought in our speech is often maya[195]; it's a kind of discharge of somebody's will or feeling. Having thoughts is something different, something more than that. Thinking makes us human, but the hardest thing is to have *real thoughts.* For everyday tasks that's fine, but in order for us to have the right kind of thoughts that are called for by the great sweep of human evolution, then it's not enough to rest content with what rises up out of feeling, let alone what rises up out of the will. We have to raise our thinking up into the sunlight of something even higher. To put it concretely: we don't just need to allow the sequence of the several cultures to exert their effect upon our souls in the way that they unfold sequentially. We also have to feel the deeper impulses that are at work within these cultural spheres. The only way to express this is through the effect of the cupola.

Hence, someone entering our building from the west and walking eastward, moving forward, will find in the sequence of the columns an expression of the will. And by feeling what rises up from below, she'll feel the European cultures and many other things besides. What will she gain from the cupola; what will approach her from the painting in the cupola? *That which lives on earth as the mysteries of the spiritual development of humanity as a whole.* Thus people's view will rise up toward this cupola, and on the one side they'll see the mysteries of the Inspiration that suffused primordial Indian culture. They'll experience how the ancient Indian Rishis[196] allowed the gifts of ancient Indian culture to flow down from the spiritual spheres. So what was meant to enter humanity, what was meant to flow into the character of the ancient Indian culture—that's something to paint in one place in the cupola. And secondly they'll be able to observe how Zarathustra gave the ancient Persian culture its characteristic stamp, fighting as it were from out of the light of the Sun against the powers of darkness. And then how the Egyptian-Babylonian-Chaldean culture gradually arises upon the physical plane, how everything is still permeated by astrological and spiritual relationships—that's what the third area of the cupola will contain.

And finally, as though standing on a precipice, the ancient Greeks, living within the culture of the nascent intellectual or mind soul; how they come to understand what it means to be human; how they are forced to solve the riddle of the Sphinx; how their solution topples the Sphinx into the abyss (which is to say, into itself)—all that will be represented in the fourth area. And the way in which the eternal, divine powers and forces affect the evolution of humanity will be expressed in something represented in terms of the four compass points, something that sits deeper than the post-Atlantean impulses in human evolution: the Atlantean or Lemurian epochs, with the genesis[197] of Atlantis at the southern end, and the genesis of Lemuria at the northern end of the cupola. And finally the upshot of Lemurian and Atlantean evolution is depicted—that which our own epoch is meant to be. Our own epoch will be depicted by the view one encounters glancing from west to east towards the smaller room. It will be expressed in the mode of depiction itself, in the impulse that runs throughout the whole of cosmic evolution[198] and that speaks itself in the "I A O."[199] Not that the I A O will be represented symbolically, but it is expressed in the motif. And if we turn our glance from east to west, then we find a correspondence there between what speaks itself out of the depths of the cosmos into the evolution of culture and the way in which the I A O speaks into the becoming of the soul from within.

But all the things I just described will be perceived only if our heads overcome the cupola that arches above our brains; only if our heads liberate their etheric bodies and look out from within, so that the things I have described will reveal themselves to us as a mighty Imagination.

The things I have described are a reality. They can be viewed clairvoyantly[200] if we free our etheric bodies from their physical basis. Then the liberated etheric brain expands out to the cosmos, and we gain a clairvoyant vision of that inner revelation. Then the whole of human earthly evolution is revealed.

Only by penetrating into the mysteries painted on the inside of our cupola will we become able to think in the right way about the phenomena of human evolution.[201] In contemplating the evolution of culture,[202] the only way to rise up into the sphere of feeling—by which I mean an unconstrained feeling that is beyond sympathy and antipathy—will be by *experiencing* what expresses itself in the motifs of the columns and architraves from below upward. By way of these motifs it will be possible to penetrate into what lives within every hour and every minute of human evolution. Only if we know what's living within the human soul at every moment of human evolution can we know what has evolved over millions of years, for everything that was contained within the Atlantean and Lemurian cultures lives within every soul. No soul would be the way it is if it hadn't assimilated all of that. The only way to understand a human soul in all its profundity is to think it within the context of earthly evolution as a whole.

So it is that our building expresses—if I may use the word "expresses"—willing, feeling, and thinking from the evolutionary perspective. It looks to what they are meant to become within human nature, which is striving for a certain self-development.[203]

Neither these forms nor the way in which we arrived at them is arbitrary. Rather, they have arisen out of the inmost depths of anthroposophical insight.

When we seek to fathom the mysteries of human nature, how often it has happened that we find ourselves confronting willing, feeling, and thinking. It's thinking, feeling, and willing that we have built with our building, and the building represents the mysterious ways in which willing, feeling, and thinking are bound together in human nature. If I go from west to east in this building, then I am moving in the way that the sphere of the human will moves itself; if I turn my gaze from below upward and contemplate the forms of the columns and architraves, then I delve down into the mysteries of the sphere of feeling within human nature. If we study what rises in the painting of the cupola above what we experience within the building, then we study the mysteries of human thinking.

You see that in a work such as our building, everything corresponds to certain inner *necessities*. Everything arises because that is how it *must* arise. That is an important part of the building's significance.

My dear friends, how is it we actually know that some Imagination, an Inspiration, or an Intuition, contains something objective? We have a sense for that because when we have an Imagination or an Inspiration or an Intuition, we have the inner experience: These things are presenting themselves not as something that has arisen *out of us*; rather, they interpolate themselves into the cosmos as a whole, and relate to the cosmos as a whole in a harmonious way. In the future, artistic concepts, aesthetic ideas[204] will need to take hold of us in such a way that we feel as an inner necessity: What has been created artistically doesn't belong to me individually; it's something that the gods create within us, for they want to have it exist in the world; they wanted it to be created; they want it to stand in the world.

You can believe with conviction that in the future, real progress within human evolution will depend upon such sensibilities and such ideas[205] taking ever greater hold. They have to replace the notions[206] that are currently popular.

Everyone who is working on this building here or is connected with this building in any way should develop a feeling that it is his or her task to compare what we intended by erecting this building, and what it expresses, with the tone that prevails generally in the world.

Making this comparison can lead to a fervent conviction,[207] which we can clarify by asking the question: How is it that the earliest forms of Christian culture arose? As I have often indicated already, all such cultural impulses have arisen in a similar way: they arose because the earliest proponents of such a cultural impulse, the first ones to stand up to be counted, were sufficiently strong in their souls to feel this impulse as all-powerful within them. What would have become of Christianity if the earliest Christians hadn't borne the Christ-impulse as all-powerful within their souls? For we know that the prevailing culture within the Roman empire above—within the part that enjoyed the physical light of day as it were—was very different from the Christian culture that developed in the dark, in little conventicles, in the catacombs, and only later climbed up into the light. And we know that nothing remains of Roman culture, and that what unfolded below in the deep darkness of the catacombs—rose up and conquered the world. That happened because down below in the catacombs it was founded within the hearts and souls of the early Christians.

Today it's not the case that we would need to hollow out the hillside in Dornach upon which we stand so that no one could see what we are doing. We didn't need to do that. We don't need to hollow out the hillside and fill it with catacombs; we don't need to hide anything. There's no need for us to prepare the new culture underground while the prevailing culture unfolds above. We don't need to do that. And yet, spiritually that is indeed the case. For how much of what we want to inscribe upon our hearts, to inscribe within our souls here, lives out there within contemporary culture? How much of what we want to express in the forms of our columns and motifs? As little as there was of early Christianity within Roman culture!

And even if we do not live in catacombs physically, spiritually we do indeed, and we have the right mood if we feel as though spiritually we are living within such catacombs. We have the right feeling for our building only if we say to ourselves in a figurative way[208]: There is the cupola of our building with its gray, gleaming slate roof, standing in the sunlight and radiating out into the surrounding countryside. But we ourselves are beneath this dome; and above all, we are beneath this dome spiritually.

That is how I wanted to characterize here again how it is someone should feel who understands the inmost impulse of anthroposophy in relationship to the outer world. Oh these early Christians, they listened to the words that resounded within their souls and their hearts, to what emanated from the Mystery of Golgotha, and they didn't fall prey to the temptations that lurked above the catacombs.

May it be so today, spiritually, within our spiritual movement! May that spirit prevail! For that qualifier "spiritually" touches on a certain difficulty. The form that this difficulty takes is that, if you contemplate the actual circumstances, sometimes it might be tempting—I say "might," not "can"—it might be tempting to wish for such a harsh and strong opposition from the outer world that we would be compelled to turn inward. We might be tempted to wish that the prevailing culture forbade us with all the means available to build anything upon this hill in Dornach; that we really would need to tunnel down into the earth and live inside, in hiding. If we were compelled to do that, we'd have a stronger feeling of the degree to which our own impulses, the impulses of anthroposophy, must be distinguished from all the fuss and bluster above.

Much can be said only figuratively, in the way I have just spoken. You must enter into the words with your feeling a bit and try to grasp their reality: then you'll begin to grasp the greater meanings to which my analogies refer.

May you take to heart everything that I discussed at length today, and all that I intended by summarizing it with these concluding words!

Lecture 5

Dornach, October 25, 1914

Yesterday we spoke about the ways in which the impulses of thinking, feeling, and willing that live within human beings should become apparent and find expression in our building.

It should be clear from many things we said over the last few days that our building should embody a new artistic element, something that did not previously exist in the evolution of humanity. This new element is crucial to human progress. Therefore we must strive to integrate it into our evolution from this moment on.

It will be difficult to understand the intention of our building merely by approaching it from the outside. The moment they try to find their way in from outside, people standing before this building will say to themselves: Well, I just can't make any sense of all that; I can't even begin to understand it. Many will come to us with conventional ideas about art and then want to criticize the building. But that's how it always has been in human history—new impulses have always been criticized from the perspective of the past.

It will help people understand the heart of the matter if we can come up with a kind of "formula" that captures in a few words what we mean when we say we want to renew the arts through a genuinely anthroposophical worldview. Looking back over the history of art, we can contemplate the architectural forms that have arisen throughout human history, in Egypt, ancient Greece, in the Gothic age. Or we can turn our attention to the kind of renewal of earlier developments we see in the Renaissance. We can contemplate the histories of painting and sculpture in the same way.

So if we consider the particular ways in which each of the arts affects our souls, and we compare it with the intentions underlying our building, then we might say that what we wanted was for something that had been at rest to be called to life. It is as though we contemplated the history of the arts and saw there a figure posed in a certain gesture, and then someone came along and said something to that person, and the figure began to walk—the figure began to move. That's how we might describe the evolution of the arts that we can follow up to our own epoch. We can look upon it as something that's standing in a resting pose, and our intention is to speak the magic word that will make it walk, bring it to life inwardly, bring it into movement. This applies to every aspect of our anthroposophical work: anthroposophy wants to meet the needs of the transformative impulses[209] that we can see everywhere in our age. It wants to seek a new element for the future evolution of humanity.

Consider just one example: a beautiful work of Greek architecture. There we see that the central concern is to create a beautiful symmetry, forms that mutually bear and support each other. But this load-bearing and supporting is static, in the same way that the individual structures of a human organism bear and support each other, as we see in a stationary figure posing before us.

Contrast that with what we intended through our own building. (In time, of course, our new impulse will have evolved beyond the primitive beginnings and the primitive means[210] with which we're compelled to work!) We have a movement that progresses from west to east; we have, as it were, motifs that grow from the simple forms that we see at the west end. The motifs of the capitals and architraves become more complicated; then they begin to turn inward and in the process they become simpler as they move in the direction of the smaller space. Something older that might be called a merely inorganic principle of symmetry has been brought into movement. Previously static structures bearing each other's weight now move. And this principle will have to find particular expression in our ideals for painting[211]—to the degree that we can accomplish it yet in our epoch.

We might say that painting has two poles. One pole is the linear and the other is the coloristic. All painting emerges from the tension between these two poles.[212] Someone can be a significant draftsman, by which I mean someone who is able to reproduce with lines the formal elements inherent within various beings,[213] someone who can deploy lines in such a way that when they're taken together an image of the inherent form[214] is called forth. But we have to be clear about one thing: anyone who lives at the linear pole of the painterly in this way has adopted a very one-sided stance toward the real or, as one often says, toward nature. For nature works not just with the lines that the painter can grasp; rather, she harbors much richer means of expressing whatever aspect of a being[215] is to be expressed. Hence a painter or a draftsman who is inwardly moved by what's harbored within a being has to be able to express more than nature can express through lines.

The linear should always awaken a specific feeling in us, namely the feeling that compared with nature herself, this linear representation remains only a surrogate. No matter how much we can accomplish through drawing, no matter how much it allows us to express, drawing never gives us anything that enables us to transcend nature. We're not even able to match nature. Our own attempts are mere bungling compared with nature herself because, with the much richer means at her disposal, nature is able to express the inner being, the essence[216] of her creations.

Hence drawing can never be more than an aid to us. And I believe that anyone who is a genuine draftsman must always be haunted by the feeling that in making a drawing one is actually just erecting the scaffolding around what really needs to be made, a scaffolding that one later takes down—and the less one sees of it later, the better!

I believe that if someone has a real artistic sensibility and looks at a painterly work of art in which drawing is especially prominent, particularly evident, she'll feel as though a scaffolding had been left standing around an otherwise finished building. This sensibility can be developed to such a degree that one always comes to feel that drawing is something which—how shall I say it—leans awkwardly upon real artistry.

Things are rather different at the other pole, the painterly or coloristic pole. But here you need to keep in mind that the coloristic is an attempt to take hold of something that actually isn't there at all in nature, or something that can be grasped only momentarily.[217] The truth of the matter is that what actually counts as coloristic is only what has been "snatched" from a being, and then painted. After all, anyone whose main concern was to imitate the sitter's clothing as realistically as possible would be a bad painter.

But actually any good painter wouldn't try to use coloration of the face to express vital relationships within the human organism. Anyone who painted a pale face—let's consider an extreme example—in order to indicate by this pallor that the sitter was perhaps inwardly ill, would actually be pursuing something that isn't genuinely artistic. Not to mention how inartistic it would be to paint a drunkard with a red nose![218]

Anyone who attempts to capture a being's static characteristics coloristically is not working in a genuinely artistic way. But if on the other hand we paint a cloud, let's say, and bring to expression in the cloud the whole magic of nature—let's say the morning sun and the way in which the morning affects the nuances of the clouds—then we've captured something that's fleeting in nature and not something that proceeds from the inwardness of an individual being, of the individual cloud. What we're grasping is something fleeting that's grounded in the relationships of the entire environment, of the cosmos, to the extent that comes into consideration. If we paint a properly illuminated cloud at a specific time of day then actually we're painting along with it the whole world as it exists at that time of day. If we paint a person and want to represent the whole of her inner constitution, then, as I've said, actually we're leaving the realm of art. But if we succeed in expressing what this person experienced—if in painting this portrait we're able to depict, for example, something that causes the person to blush, then we're already standing more within the realm of art. And even more so the moment that the picture gives us insight into the sitter's experience, when the red of the cheeks tells us what the sitter must have experienced, and so once again we're dealing not with the inner life of a being but rather with what's in the whole environment, in the whole cosmos.

What I'm saying now is related in a certain way to what I said in my lectures on *Inner Reading and Inner Hearing*.[219] There I described how, in waking consciousness, the soul is actually always outside the body, and our body is only a mirror that we use to bring to consciousness what lives outside in the cosmos.[220] The only way to be a real artist is to live with things out in the cosmos; for the real artist, the motif is only an occasion for representing her own life within the larger cosmos.

Returning to our previous example, if we paint a cloud, then actually we're outside the clouds with everything we're feeling and thinking,[221] and the cloud is only the occasion for projecting upon an individual being what lives within the cosmos as a whole. But if we want to live within the cosmos with regard to the coloristic, then we need to awaken the colors to life. After all, colors present themselves to us as qualities of beings within the natural world outside us. If we observe strictly at the level of the physical plane, we come to recognize colors through natural objects. If we want to see color, we always need a substrate, with one exception: the atmospheric phenomenon of the rainbow. That's why the phenomenon of the rainbow has rightly been viewed as something that connects the heavens—the spiritual—with the earth.[222] In viewing the rainbow, we're seeing not a colored sky but rather color as such.

In earlier lectures,[223] I described that it's possible to delve down into a realm of flowing color, to live with the colors—to liberate them, as it were, from objects and to live with the color. When we emancipate colors from objects and live with the colors, this realm of color reveals deep mysteries. A whole world lives in the ebbing and flowing sea of color.

Then the need arises to liberate the world of color from the conditions that have been imposed upon it on the physical plane. Then the need arises to seek the creativity at work within the colors.[224]

If the painting in our building is to be integrated organically into the edifice as a whole, then the painting that we allow to unfold within this building has to be animated by this impulse. Especially within the coloristic element, we must strive to represent the life of color as it transcends the physical plane, where everything colored (with the exception of the rainbow and other such phenomena) is fixed by objects. For example, it has to become possible for our souls to live so completely within blue that it's as though nothing else existed in the world, as though there were only that blue, and we feel as though poured out into this blue that fills the whole world.

But what will happen if we enter in the right way into this flowing, undulating realm of color is not the same as applying a layer of color; rather, we enter into the creative activity of color itself. What we find when we enter into the creative activity of color itself is something inwardly differentiated. If we live within blue, for example, and gradually find our way into it, we find that blue has something that attracts our soul; it is as though our soul wants to lose itself within the blue—we yearn for it, ever and again. And we see forms arising out of the blue, forms that bring to expression the mysteries of the cosmos, forms that bring to expression the soul of the cosmos. Out of the creative activity of color itself a world shall arise, a world that configures itself, that differentiates itself inwardly, that becomes substantial.[225] Form shall be born of color. We shall feel not only that we're living within the color, but also that the color is giving birth to form, and thus that form is the work of color.[226]

So it is that by way of color we can live our way into the creative force at the foundation of the world. The only way that can happen is if we paint in such a way that we don't merely cover a surface, but rather point outward toward the life of the cosmos as a whole, participate[227] in the life of the entire cosmos. In this way we will have to grasp inwardly what I characterized yesterday as a necessary component of our cupola paintings—the impulses of Lemurian, Atlantean, and post-Atlantean life as expressed in the Ancient Indian, Ancient Persian, Egypto-Chaldean, and Greco-Roman cultures. Out of this inward grasping of color,[228] which shall simultaneously become the grasping of form[229] as it flows into our work, we shall comprehend what lives within the evolution of humanity.

Anyone who studies the earlier history of painting to date will see that the tendency has been to live within color, within the coloristic, in the way that color is affixed to objects on the physical plane. The ideal of the painting in the cupolas of our building must be to free color, to emancipate color from objects. The heart of the matter is that we have to turn the whole impulse of painting sharply inward and bring it into movement.[230]

It will be difficult to make our intentions comprehensible to our contemporaries. We will simply have to forego that for the time being, because as long as it is still possible for someone to judge a work of art "correct" or "good" or whatever because it reminds him of something real, nobody will be able to understand our paintings. As long as people can still say that a tree has been painted well if it is as naturalistic as possible, that it seems to them as though they were standing in front of a real tree—as long as this is the criterion for judging painting and the arts generally, nobody will be able to understand anything about the kind of painting we should be doing. The kind of painting that is our ideal will be taken for foolishness; people will be able to make nothing of it. For they'll ask: Why is it that works of art were always there? To be viewed of course! And who would ever have thought that works of art were there for any other reason than to be viewed? But the art we're striving to create in our building won't be there to be viewed, not at all! And we can be glad that people who believe after all their preliminaries and studies that works of art are there to be viewed could not think less of our artwork. For one thing is certain: what these people don't want is exactly what we want to have!

We have had some specific experiences that are entirely symptomatic. One of our friends once met me on the path from the Glass House to our home and recounted a conversation with an elderly gentleman who reportedly said: If the person who designed these cupolas had ever seen St. Peter's in Rome, he would've done these cupolas differently. Well, the person who designed these cupolas has seen St. Peter's not just once but many times! He was able to take joy from it, and to feel the grandeur of St. Peter's. But for all that he designed the cupolas just as they are.

It's entirely natural for us to encounter such judgments, because St. Peter's was made to be viewed. But the things we're making here aren't just to be viewed—they're meant to be really experienced. And what should have been the answer to this elderly gentleman? The right answer would have been to say to him: Do you know the fairy tale about the prince ...[231] who always looked at everything through his window? And you know what happened one day when he had to "eat of the serpent"? Then he began to understand what the sparrows on the roof and the chickens in the courtyard were saying to each other. The old man apparently had not "eaten of the serpent." What does that mean exactly, "to eat of the serpent"? It means that you haven't just peeked theoretically into anthroposophy, but rather allowed it to take hold of your entire soul and inmost heart, so that you feel an image of anthroposophy alive within you. If you can feel it with your whole soul, then you've "eaten of the serpent," and then you've experienced the ideal of our building. You don't just look at it, you experience the intention underlying it; you find one way of experiencing how dull and unconscious we are in our wills as we pass from incarnation to incarnation—when we're born into this culture in one incarnation and that culture in another.

Just as our building lets you experience the impulses of the human will as you progress from west to east following the succession of the motifs of the columns, capitals, and architraves, you can experience the element of human feeling in what develops upward from below. But you need to experience it! And the element of thinking—the place where thinking is no longer merely abstract, cold and sober, but is animated by the heart of the cosmos itself—that is something you should experience through the way in which the cupolas complete and enclose the space. You have to experience it in all the details of the cupola. So, for example, when a color is juxtaposed with another color that is never next to it in nature; when a being that has human-like features in its countenance appears there colored in a way that it could never appear in nature, then you have to experience how that which comes to expression there, the inner aspect, has been brought to vital expression.

If we can succeed to any degree, then a start will have been made in experiencing painting as an expression not of nature but of the spirit.[232] Even if it is just a beginning. Nothing may imitate nature, above all in painting.

Two ideals must be attained in our building that only a very few people are just beginning to cherish. It is truly detrimental that so many people want to hear nothing about the great vistas of humanity's future evolution. You see, if you wish to find in concentrated form[233] everything of which our building is meant to be the symbol,[234] then you have to come alive in your soul; you have to enliven your soul by means of all kinds of feelings. You can't express what was intended there in one simple, easily comprehensible sensation. Rather, you have to try to collate what your soul should actually be sensing out of the many different dimensions of the feeling-life of the world.

Consider epochs other than our own. Let's think about the horizon of ancient Greece, not to mention earlier times, and let's consider especially all the things that didn't exist yet for the Greeks but exist for us today. What wasn't there yet for the Greeks? Well, America and Australia were unknown to them. They knew nothing of the Western Hemisphere of the earth. And they were also ignorant of many things that we know now about Europe, Asia, and Africa. Geographically, the Greeks' horizon was a narrow one. Try to put yourself in the shoes of a Greek looking at the map that was available to him. Try that, and then try to shift your thoughts to the rich world that the Greeks inhabited; direct your thoughts to everything that was creative within the Greeks. Try to compare the geographical map of the heavens that the Greeks were able to draw with our celestial maps today. The map of the physical configuration of the earth was quite small, but in comparison the map of the heavens was very large. The ancient Greeks still possessed something that was essentially a spiritual experience of the physical plane: geographically, tightly constricted; spiritually, gazing out into great heavenly vistas.

The experience of the Greeks was, for example, no longer that of the Egypto-Babylonian-Chaldean epoch, during which it was still possible to look out into the cosmos and to experience in their astrological ideas[235] something of the actual spiritual beings, of whom the constellations are the physical expression. But a kind of residue of all that was still present in ancient Greece. When we read in Homer's *Iliad* that Thetis tells Achilles that Zeus can't intervene because he is in Ethiopia and won't return to his house for twelve days,[236] that account still bears a relationship to astrology, but the depiction is such that the reader doesn't notice the idea of progression through the Zodiac underlying the passage. When the Greeks said, "Zeus went off to feast with the Ethiopians," they meant that he was located within a certain sign of the zodiac. The number twelve also indicates that. All of this already bears the coloration of what's yet to come, but on the other hand it's still saturated by what humanity originally experienced as the breadth of the spiritual horizon.

Now let's turn our gaze away from the Greeks and direct it toward the modern age. The sphere of the earth rounds itself out geographically to an ever greater extent, and today very few areas remain that are, so to speak, entirely blank spaces upon the globe. We witness the advent of modernity. Asian cultures have integrated America into their maps—the same America that was still completely absent for the Greeks. The geographical horizon becomes ever greater, but the spiritual horizon, the map of the heavens as it were, shrivels up completely. What does modern humanity know about the inhabitants of Greek mythology? We no longer know anything about it! There's a fundamental sense in which the soul of European civilization feeds upon the history of Greek culture. (As for the history that predates Greece, even where documents are available it feels spectral to historians.) If people assimilate the elements of Greek antiquity that are offered in schools today, then the history that they assimilate, the history in which our souls are living, is only the one they've learned externally. We really drag quite a bit of history around with us, really quite a bit.

This isn't the case with Asians, nor is it the case with today's Americans. Americans have their own kind of history, a history that stands, so to speak, outside of life itself. Europeans live much more historically than Americans do.

I imagine that few Americans will put much stake in tracing back their family trees for centuries. Probably very few. But in Europe the number of people who wish to do so is large. That's what I mean by lugging history around, and it has important consequences for the way life is lived—even social life.

A distant future is conceivable—and for clairvoyants it's more than just conceivable—in which everything that we drag around with us in the way of history since Greek antiquity has gone to sleep. Let's not talk about where it is sleeping; it is possible to imagine a time when a great wave will have swept from Asia over Europe and America, after which people will know on the physical plane as little about the European history we now narrate and experience as we know today about what happened in Europe four to six thousand years ago. We can look forward to the time in which this cultural wave will have swept through Asia, in which a form of life very different from ours today will have developed and where the things that move us today in the innermost fiber of our being lie like deposits in geological layers. Then all that will be as much a part of the past as the things that happened upon European soil three, four, five thousand years ago are for us.

The time will come when, shall we say, Goethe will be discovered in the same way that we today have discovered the ancient world in the earliest Egyptian hieroglyphs, in the way we've discovered what happened back then. For there will be people who feel the need to discover Goethe in this way, outwardly and physically.[37]

And here we see a remarkable vista opening up before us within human evolution. Just as the ancient Greeks knew nothing of America, the descendants of today's Americans will know about the Greeks only as something long forgotten—or in some sense know nothing about them, in the way I have described.

What I've just described as more of a physical process also has a kind of spiritual counterpart. The spiritual counterpart unfolds in such a way that, in the future, humanity will have to develop a new capacity to discover the spiritual world and to know it. The spiritual world is as much *terra incognita* for most people today as America was for the Greeks. We're just beginning voyages of discovery, voyages to discover the America of the spirit. Spiritually, we stand right where the Europeans stood when the first ships set sail for America. Inwardly, we are on a voyage to discover the other half—the spiritual half—of human existence.

All of these things were meant to give only a hint of the meaning and the import of anthroposophy for human evolution. Every one of you can flesh out yourself the parts of this sketch that remain incomplete. Suppose for a moment that America hadn't been discovered, and that Europeans were still living in ignorance of America. Is that conceivable? No, it's totally inconceivable! In the same way a time will come when it will be inconceivable that human beings might not have been able to discover the spiritual world in the sense of anthroposophy. It will be utterly inconceivable.

But this comparison can be spun out further. What attended upon the geographical expansion of human consciousness? If we search through all the previous cultures in human history for the culture that was most spiritual, and embodied that ideal completely, then we have to look for such a culture before the discovery of America, because the discovery of America coincides with the beginnings of materialism. All geographical expansions are mysteriously connected with the spread of materialism. Humanity has to find its way back to an ideal, spiritual knowledge of the world. We will find it by discovering the America of the spirit, and that's something we'll discover when we find embodied in the world the path that we have already symbolized in our building.

We had to indicate the progressive direction[238] of our building by going from column to column, and from motif to motif within the architraves. Here the progress was on the physical plane. But we must add to this that it is possible to look up; that we can follow the motifs upwards from below; that we can look upward.

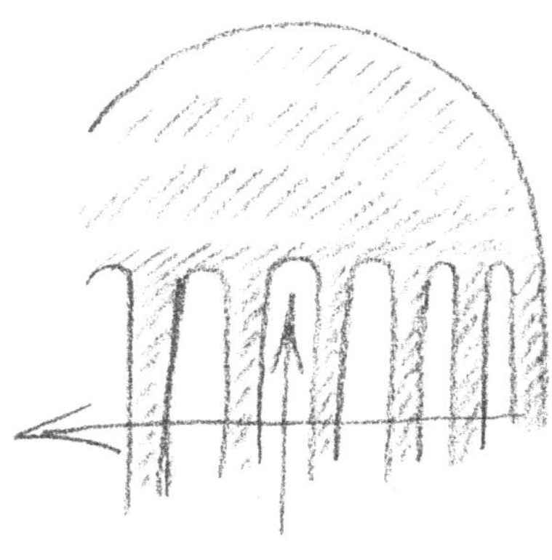

FIG. 14

History reveals a kind of progress, a kind of forward movement, on the physical plane—I mean the unfolding of history that we can observe outwardly. But humanity will have to undergo a deepening of the soul that actually, like Faust's descent to the Mothers, represents an ascent into the spiritual world.[239] This deepening of the soul is of course simultaneously a rising up into spiritual worlds, which is called forth by the spiritual powers of the Good.

But this ascent into the spiritual world will bring with it a kind of closure. A kind of *closure*, I say. Please take that word exactly the way I meant it. Nowadays when people talk about evolution, the idea they have is something like a barrel that begins rolling, and rolls on and on and on, but at the same time they imagine that it never actually began rolling; it has just always been rolling. Anyone who talks about evolution today imagines that evolution was always there, as though everything just evolved on and on and on, and that everything has always just been this way and that way. But that's not how things really are. It's just a bad habit, a lack of intellectual sophistication when we think of evolution extending endlessly into the past and into the future. The earth is evolving—geographically, physically—and every culture is evolving as well. But one day the end will come, a conclusion when everything has been discovered, and then there will be closure. Then we won't be able to say to ourselves: Now let's fit out our ships and discover more things. That doesn't work. It's just not true that evolution can go on forever: evolution has a conclusion. And just as physical evolution has to reach a conclusion, spiritual evolution must also attain closure. Someday a cupola really will rise up above everything humanity has experienced historically. And although it's true that no one will be able any longer to fit out ships in order to discover even more remote lands of the Earth, because the whole globe has been discovered, it is equally true that one day all the things humanity can discover spiritually will also have been discovered. It would be an entirely false idea[240] of evolution if we were to say to ourselves: Well, humanity has already discovered so much, researched so many things, it'll always perform more and more research, endlessly, and it'll always discover new things. That would be the worst idea[241] we could cultivate. After all we need to think in accordance with reality if we want to arrive at good ideas.[242] But few people indeed are able to think in accordance with reality today; they believe they're thinking real thoughts, but they aren't. You can find people nowadays who say for example: Well, when there's nothing left to investigate, then the world will be a very boring place, because, after all, that's what makes life interesting, precisely the fact that we can't imagine inquiry ever ending. But there will be an end one day, just as there will be an end of geographical discovery. And to anyone who suffers at the thought of humanity no longer having research to do, and asks what humanity would do with its time—to these people we must reply: Humanity will do something other than research, it will sort that all out.

Now you might ask: What's the point of this train of thought?[243] But if you conjoin these ideas,[244] you can arrive at the answer yourself. We see that, in a way, the whole history of human life plays itself out in the way that our building rises up and arches over us. Humanity progresses through the turning points of time when we move from column to column; humanity raises itself up in the way that our gaze rises up to the capitals of the columns and the architraves; and humanity hopes for a consummation in the way that we find closure when we look up into the interior of the cupola.

And we should feel a kind of consummation there. Just as history will be consummated, the painting of our cupola will also create closure. This painting should not be such that it merely covers the surface. Rather it should call forth the thought that if you lift up your gaze to the painting on the surface of the cupola, then you'll find nothing [physical] there. You should forget the material substrate of the painting that's there. The paintings should be transparent; you have to look through what's painted [on the surfaces][245] there, look through them out into the expanses of the Spirit.

Perhaps we won't be able to accomplish this with our present building, but as the principle underlying our building is developed further, eventually humanity will attain it. In the future, humanity will look upon what it has received from anthroposophy as a mighty cupola—a cupola whose configuration guides them outward into the infinity of spiritual life.

Yes, my dear friends, when we're living at one place on the Earth and we want to travel to another, but at certain times we're not able to do so,[246] then it hits home to us that, yes, people are hostile to each other, that they argue over the things of the Earth—indeed, more than argue. But people can't fight over the Sun and the stars. Even though the Chinese call their ruler "the son of the Sun," "the son of Heaven," and even though they have begun many wars with other people on Earth—they never started a war over possession of the Sun. It never occurred to them to contend with other peoples over possession of the Sun. No end of things can give the peoples of the Earth occasion for strife and war. But that which directs our gaze upward to the spiritual world *cannot* be the occasion for conflict. It never can lead to strife and war.

Now we have to be clear that many things must still unfold in the course of earthly evolution before humanity will have come so far as to be able to see into the spiritual world in this way through anthroposophy. What anthroposophy offers should be like what the Sun and the stars are to physical life. But many things are needed before that can happen. What is needed above all is that through anthroposophy we begin to think not just with the instrument people mostly use today—not just with our heads. And in a certain sense we can say: Nothing is more foreign to us than our head. Really, nothing is more foreign to us than our head! For the essential basis[247] of what has become the human head was already finished at the time of Old Sun evolution.[248] The rest is an inheritance—partly from Saturn evolution—that has evolved further, and was subject to an important intervention during Moon evolution. The things that are thought in the head are, fundamentally, as foreign to us as our contemporary cognition is remote from Old Saturn, Old Sun, and Old Moon evolution.

Colloquial sayings often contain deep truths. But don't ever believe the common saying that everyone has their own head![249] That's false! None of us has our own head; everyone has the mind of the entire cosmos! It would be truer to say that each of us has our own heart. But to claim that each of us has our own mind is nonsensical.

We need to begin to develop a kind of thinking that's actually an experience, like the inner experience of standing up I described yesterday. We actually experience standing up only with our heads. We really experience it very abstractly, that colossal thing unfolding within us when we raise ourselves out of a recumbent position, in which we're more or less parallel to the surface of the earth, into the orientation of the radius of the earth.[250] This change, this reorientation from the horizontal beam to the vertical beam of the Cross as it were—if we really experience it, then we experience something totally colossal. We experience something cosmic: the cosmic Cross.

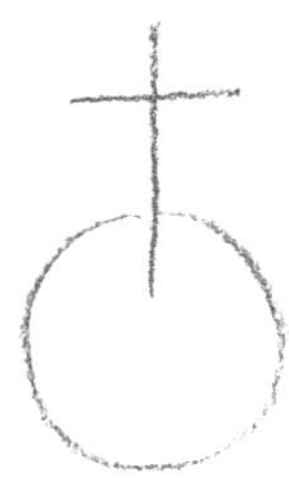

Fig. 15

We experience this every day, but we don't reflect every day that as soon as we begin moving, this cross is inscribed into our very lives. It's inscribed every time we stand up and lie down.

But this abstract standing up and lying down, this assumption of the form of the Cross, is still a very far cry from an idea[251] that we can express by saying: If human beings were not related to the Earth such that they lie down and stand up again, then the Mystery of Golgotha would not have been a necessary event in the evolution of the world.[252]

If someone speaks the sound "b" or writes the letter "b," then that signifies the sound "b." And if we asked how to spell "Earth" in a way that expresses the fact that the Mystery of Golgotha was necessary for human evolution, then the answer would be the sign of the Cross, which conjoins our lying down and our standing up. Because human beings lie and stand upon the Earth, human nature as a whole is such that the Mystery of Golgotha had to occur.

If we would begin to think with our "second brain"—not with the brain in our head,[253] but with the second brain (I described this in my lectures on *Inner Reading and Inner Hearing*[254] by saying that we have to view the lobes of our brains like arms that are held fast, the way it would be if our arms and hands coalesced with our torso and so forth)—if we use our "second brain," then we'll begin to think in such a way that the sign of the Cross is beyond any doubt the symbol for the Mystery of Golgotha. But our "head-brain" is not well suited[255] to this kind of thinking yet. Many misunderstandings in the world arise from the use of this brain. The reason why so many misunderstandings arise is because it is still only this "head-brain" that's creative. The "second brain" has to become creative as well—become creative to such a degree that something is accomplished in the world that's captured in a certain sense by the image I just placed before you. I said that the Greeks didn't know America. But if we have recourse to other records,[256] then we find that there were indeed times in which America was known. It's just that knowledge of America was lost again. In the same way, there were times when things were known that anthroposophy now strives to recover.[257] Anthroposophy teaches us that much has to be regained consciously that was previously known to humanity in a dreamy way, out of unconscious experiences. Humanity really did share a kind of common language that later differentiated itself. The myth of the Tower of Babel has a profoundly real basis. But as long as human beings think only with their heads, they won't be able to think creatively; they won't be creative in the way that earlier people were for example with respect to language.[258] But anthroposophy bears an inherent propensity to bring the whole element of language into creative movement.[259] I said with reference to our building that it had brought the artistic element into movement, but it also has to be said that life itself must be brought into movement.

We can gaze into a distant future in which anthroposophy will be creative, a time when everything we think and imagine[260] will make language itself creative. Just as anthroposophy will someday be spread over the whole of the Earth, so also will it call forth a common language that corresponds to none of our contemporary languages. Not like Volapük[261] or Esperanto,[262] for those languages arose externally, artificially.[263] The language of the future will arise when humanity learns to live within the sounds of speech, just as we can learn to live within color.

If we can learn to live within sounds, then sound itself will give birth to the configuration, so that humanity regains the possibility of creating a language out of spiritual experience again. Although we still might stand at the beginning with regard to many aspects of anthroposophy, with regard to the things I just characterized we're not even beginners. But we have to begin thinking about these things in order to feel the full import and the essence of anthroposophy in our souls. We have to begin to feel that anthroposophy bears within its bosom the seeds not only of a new knowledge, but also of a new art and even of a new language. This language will not be constructed; rather, we shall give birth to it.

Just as humanity never will quarrel over the Sun and the stars, it never will quarrel over this new language. The older languages will carry on quite nicely; they'll continue to exist after this new language has arisen.

As you can already feel, no doubt, what I just said represents a very distant goal; we're cherishing quite a remote ideal. And most of the materialistic thinkers of today would surely respond to what I've just said by exclaiming: That's just pie in the sky;[264] the fool who said all those things about the creative element in language and about anthroposophy is just building castles in the air.

You can easily imagine such derision directed toward us from this or that corner, some great eminence in the eyes of today's world ridiculing the way we have our heads in the clouds and no ground beneath our feet. The charge can even make sense to us, because when we have set forth such high ideals, we really have left the ground beneath our feet. As long as the Earth continues to evolve as a physical planet, this ideal shall not arrive. The Earth shall pass away before this ideal is realized. But human souls shall be resurrected into other planetary embodiments, and they shall experience the realization of this ideal if they become conscious of this ideal just now, in our own day.

Indeed, Ahriman himself could stand there and judge between us and the eminence listening and laughing in the corner because he thinks we have lost the ground beneath our feet. Then Ahriman could rub his hands together and say: That's what they call future ideals; they've lost the ground beneath their feet—the man over there says it. But the joke's on him and he doesn't know it; he speaks the truth and knows it not.

But we know: Even if we aren't standing on firm ground, we stand within reality itself when we make these ideas the most living word within our souls. And why is that? Because we profess our faith in the Mystery of Golgotha, not in the thoughtless way that is so common today but rather with deep earnestness. We know that Christ lives, and that we can know the truth if we allow Him to become our great teacher and guide with regard to spiritual wisdom.

Christ made a pronouncement, which says: You can confess me in your innermost soul only if you transcend those words and those ideals that shall pass away with the Earth—the whole outer configuration of the Earth shall pass away, and shall not remain as it now is—you can confess me only if you listen to my words. And of these words, He Himself said: "Heaven and earth shall pass away, but my words shall not pass away."[265] And so it is that we can stand firm in our souls, my dear friends, even though we confess ideals that seem to our opponents like castles in the air. If we want to confess the Mystery of Golgotha, then we must confess those ideals that are more lasting than the Earth and all the constellations of the heavens that circle the Earth in the cosmos. Then we must attend to the revelations of the Mystery of Golgotha, which shall remain even when the Earth itself no longer remains, nor even the heavens, which now look down upon the Earth.

The meaning of these words proceeding from the Mystery of Golgotha is profound, truly profound. And the ones who are living an illusion are those who are unwilling to raise themselves up from the earth into this cupola that is meant to become transparent and look into the spiritual world. For if this cupola is meant to be the expression of the Mystery of Golgotha within architecture, then it must itself speak to us a language that can remind us of the saying:

> Heaven and earth shall pass away,
> but my words shall not pass away.

5. *Preparation and carving work in the carpenter's workshop, May 1914*

6. *Carving work on the curvatures between the columns and the internal wall*

7. *Carving the capitals in the concrete underbody of the building, April 1914*

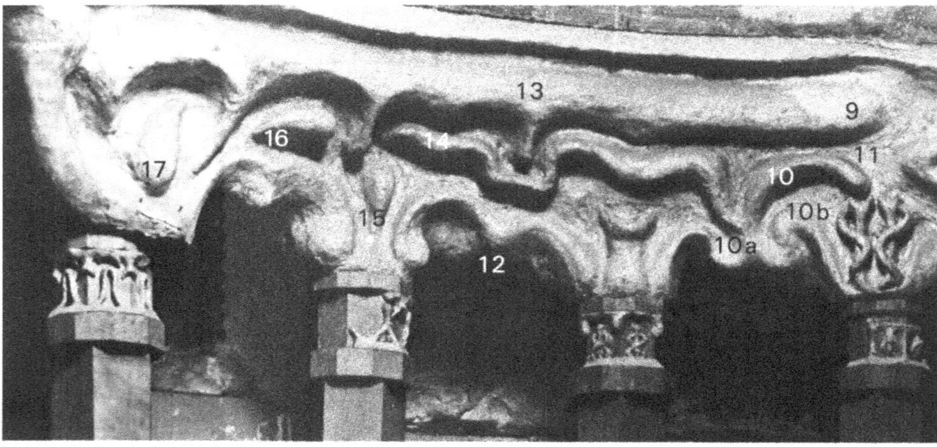

8. *Architrave of the large dome, model*

9. *Architrave of the large dome, status of the carving work in October 1914*

8
4
1
6
3
2

10. *Large dome space of the first Goetheanum: seventh to fourth column*

11. *Large dome space of the first Goetheanum: fourth to first column*

12. *Construction workers assembling the capitals*

APPENDIX

"A Reply to Prof. Harnack by Some British Theologians"

Prof. Harnack
Honored Sir:

We, the undersigned, a group of theologians who owe more than we can express to you personally and to the great host of German teachers and leaders of thought, have noticed with pain a report of a speech recently delivered by you, in which you are said to have described the conduct of Great Britain in the present war as that of a traitor to civilization.

We are quite sure that you could never have been betrayed into such a statement if you had been acquainted with the real motives which actuate the British Nation in the present crisis.

Permit us, in the interests of a better understanding now and subsequently, to state to you the grounds on which we, whose obligations to Germany, personal and professional, are simply incalculable, have felt it our duty to support the British Government in its declaration of war against the land and people we love so well.

We are not actuated by any preference for France over Germany—still less by any preference for Russia over Germany. The preference lies entirely the other way. Next to the peoples that speak the English tongue, there is no people in the world that stands so high in our affection and admiration as the people of Germany. Several of us have studied in German universities. Many of us have enjoyed warm personal friendship with your fellow-countrymen. All of us owe an immeasurable debt to German theology, philosophy, and literature. Our sympathies are in matters of the spirit so largely German that nothing but the very strongest reasons could ever lead us to contemplate the possibility of hostile relations between Great Britain and Germany.

Nor have we the remotest sympathy with any desire to isolate Germany, or to restrict her legitimate expansion, commercial and colonial. We have borne resolute witness against the endeavor made by foes of Germany to foment anti-German suspicion and ill-will in the minds of our fellow-countrymen.

The Sanctity of Treaties

But we recognize that all hopes of settled peace between the nations, and indeed of any civilized relations between the nations, rest on the maintenance inviolate of the sanctity of treaty obligations. We can never hope to put law for war if solemn international compacts can be torn up at the will of any power involved. These obligations are felt by us to be the more stringently binding in the case of guaranteed neutrality. For the steady extension of neutralization appears to us to be one of the surest ways of the progressive elimination of war from the face of the earth. All these considerations take on a more imperative cogency when the treaty rights of a small people are threatened by a great world power. We therefore believe that when Germany refused to respect the neutrality of Belgium, which she herself had guaranteed, Great Britain had no option, either in international law or in Christian ethics, but to defend the people of Belgium. The Imperial Chancellor of Germany has himself admitted, on Aug. 4, that the protest of the Luxembourg and Belgian Governments was "just," and that Germany was doing "wrong" and acting "contrary to the dictates of international law." His only excuse was "necessity"—which recalls our Milton's phrase, "necessity, the tyrant's plea." It has cost us all the deepest pain to find the Germany which we love so intensely committing this act of lawless aggression on a weak people, and a Christian nation becoming a mere army with army ethics. We loathe war of any kind. A war with Germany cuts us to the very quick. But we sincerely believe that Great Britain in this conflict is fighting for conscience, justice, Europe, humanity, and lasting peace.

Dictated Terms

This conviction is deepened by the antecedents of the present unhappy war. In allowing her ally Austria to dictate terms to Serbia which were quite incompatible with the independence of that little State, Germany gave proof of her disregard for the rights of smaller States. A similar disregard for the sovereign rights of greater States was shown in the demand that Russia should demobilize her forces. It was quite open to Germany to have answered Russia's mobilization with a counter-mobilization without resorting to war. Many other nations have mobilized to defend their frontiers without declaring war. Alike indirectly in regard to Serbia and directly in regard to Russia, Germany was indisputably the aggressor. And this policy of lawless aggression became more nakedly manifest in the invasion of Belgium. Great Britain is not bound by any treaty rights to defend either Serbia or Russia. But she is bound by the most sacred obligations to defend Belgium, obligations which France undertook to observe. We have been grieved to the heart to see in the successive acts of German policy a disregard of the liberties of States, small or great, which is the very negation of civilization. It is not our country that has incurred the odium of being a traitor to civilization or to the conscience of humanity.

Doubtless you read the facts of the situation quite differently. You may think us entirely mistaken. But we desire to assure you, as fellow-Christians and fellow-theologians, that our motives are not open to the charge which has been made.

We have been moved to approach you on this matter by our deep reverence for you and our high appreciation of the great services you have rendered to Christendom in general. We trust that you will receive what we have said in the spirit in which it was sent.

We have the honor to be,

Yours very sincerely,

P.J. FORSYTH, M.A., D.D., Aberdeen University. Principal of Hackney College (Divinity School: University of London)

HERBERT T. ANDREWS, B.A. Oxon. Professor of New Testament, Exegesis, Introduction and Criticism. New College, London (Divinity School: University of London)

J. HERBERT DARLOW, M.A. Cambridge. Literary Superintendent of the British and Foreign Bible Society

JAMES R. GILLIES, M.A. Edinburgh, Moderator of the Presbyterian Church of England. Pastor of Hampstead Presbyterian Church, London

R. MACLEOD, Pastor of Frognal Presbyterian Church, London.

W.M. MACPHAIL, M.A. Glasgow. General Secretary of the Presbyterian Church of England

RICHARD ROBERTS, Pastor of Crouch Hill Presbyterian Church, London

H.H. SCULLARD, M.A. Cambridge, M.A., D.D. London. Professor of Ecclesiastical History, Christian Ethics, and the History of Religions in New College (University of London)

ALEX RAMSAY, M.A., B.D. Pastor of the Highgate Presbyterian Church, London

W.B. SELBIE, M.A., D.D. Principal of Mansfield College, Oxford. Chairman of the Congregational Union of England and Wales

J. HERBERT STEAD, M.A. Glasgow. Warden of the Robert Browning Settlement, London

"Prof. Harnack in Rebuttal"

BERLIN, Sept. 10, 1914.

Gentlemen:

The words, "The conduct of Great Britain is that of a traitor to civilization," were not used by me, but you have expressed my general judgment of this conduct correctly. The sentence in question in my speech reads: "This, our culture, the chief treasure of mankind, was in large part, yes, almost wholly, entrusted to three peoples: To us, to the Americans, and—to the English, I will say no more. I cover my head." To my deep sorrow I must, even after your communication, maintain this judgment.

You claim that England has drawn and must draw the sword purely for the protection of the small nations of Serbia and Belgium and for the sake of an international treaty. In this claim I see at the very least a fearful self-delusion.

It is an actual fact that what Serbia desired was that her Government should in no wise be mixed up with the shameful crime of Sarajevo, and it is also an established fact that for years Serbia, with the support of Russia, has attempted by the most despicable means to incite to rebellion the Austrian South Slavs. When Austria finally issued to her a decided ultimatum without making any actual attack on her territory, it was the duty of every civilized land—England as well—to keep hands off, for Austria's royal house, Austria's honor, and Austria's existence were attacked. Austria's yielding to Serbia would mean the sovereignty of Russia in the eastern half of the Balkans, for Serbia is nothing more than a Russian satrapy, and the Balkan federation brought about by Russia had for its ultimate purpose opposition to Austria. This is as well known in England as in Germany. If, gentlemen, in spite of this, you can presume to judge that in this circumstance it was purely a case of protecting the right of a small nation against a large one, I shall find great difficulty in believing in your good faith.

Against Pan-Slavism

It was not a question of little Serbia but of Austria's battle for life and the struggle of Western culture against Pan-Slavism. Serbia is, after all, only an outpost of Russia and as opposed to this nation, Serbia's "sovereignty" is less than a mere shadow; in fact it can hardly be protected by England, for in reality it does not exist. For in addition Serbia, through the most dastardly murder known to history, struck her name from the list of the nations with which one does business as equals. What would England have done had the Prince of Wales been assassinated by the emissary of a little nation which had continually been inciting the Irish to revolt? Would it have issued a milder ultimatum than Austria's? But of all this you say not a word in your communication, but instead persist on seeing in the situation into which Serbia and Russia have brought Austria, only the necessity of an oppressed little country to whose help haste must be made! Thus to judge would be more than blindness, indeed, it would be a crime that cries unto heaven, were it not known that the life problems of other great powers do not exist for Great Britain, because she is only concerned about her own life problems and those of little nations whose support can be useful to her.

At bottom Serbia is of as little consequence to you as to us. Austria, too, is of no consequence to you; and you realize that Austria had the right to punish Serbia. But because Germany, who stands behind Austria, is to be struck; therefore Serbia is the guiltless little State which must be spared! What is the result? Great Britain sides with Russia against Germany. What does that mean? That means that Great Britain has torn down the dike which has protected West Europe and its culture from the desert sands of the Asiatic barbarism of Russia and of Pan-Slavism. Now we Germans are forced to stop up the breach with our bodies. We shall do it amid streams of blood, and we shall hold out there. We must hold out, for we are protecting the labor of thousands of years for all of Europe, and for Great Britain! But that day when Great Britain tore down the dam will never be forgotten in the history of the world, and history's judgment shall read: On that day when Russian-Asiatic power rushed down upon the culture of Europe Great Britain declared that she must side with Russia because "the sovereignty of the murderer-nation Serbia had been violated!"

As to Neutrality

But no, the maintenance of Serbians sovereignty is not according to your communication the first, but only the second reason for Great Britain's declaration of war against us. The first reason is our violation of Belgian neutrality; "Germany broke a treaty which she herself had guaranteed." Shall I remind you how Great Britain has disported herself in the matter of treaties and pleasant promises? How about Egypt for example? But I do not need to go into these flagrant and repeated violations of treaty rights, for a still more serious violation of the rights of a people stands today on your books against you; it has been proved that your army is making use of dumdum bullets and thereby turning a decent war into the most bloody butchery. In this Great Britain has severed herself from every right to complain about the violation of the rights of a people.

But aside from that—in your communication you have again emphasized the main point. We did not declare war against Belgium, but we declared that since Russia and France compelled us to wage a war with two fronts (190,000,000 against 68,000,000) we had then to suffer defeat if we could not march through Belgium; that we should do that but that we should carefully keep from harming Belgium in any way and would indemnify all damage incurred—our hand upon it! Would Great Britain, had she been in our position, have hesitated a moment to do likewise? And would Great Britain have drawn the sword for us if France had violated the neutrality of Belgium by marching through it? You know well enough that both these questions must be answered in the negative.

Our Imperial Chancellor has with his characteristic conscientiousness declared that we have on our side committed a certain wrong. I cannot agree with him in this judgment, and I cannot even recognize the commission of a formal wrong, for we were in a situation where formalities no longer obtain, and where moral duties only prevail. When David, in the extremity of his need, took the show-bread from the Table of the Lord, he was in every sense of the word justified, for the letter of the law ceased at that moment to exist. It is as well known to you as to me that there is a law of necessity which breaks iron asunder, to say nothing of treaties.

Appreciate our position! Prove to me that Germany has flippantly constructed a law of necessity; prove it to me in this hour, when your country has gone over to our enemies, and we have half the world to fight. You cannot do that; you could not do it on the 4th of August, and consequently you have assumed the most miserable of pretexts, because you wished to destroy us. From your letter, gentlemen, I must believe that you are far from holding this view; but do you believe, and would you really try to make me believe, that your statesmen would have declared war against us only because we were determined to march through Belgium? You could not consider them so foolish and so flippant.

An Earlier Treachery

But I am not yet at an end. It is not we who have first violated the neutrality of Belgium. Belgium, as we feared and as we now, informed by the actual facts, see still more clearly, was for a long time in alliance with France and—with you. France's airmen were flying over Belgium before we marched in; negotiations with France had already taken place, and in Maubeuge there was found an arsenal full of English munitions which had been stationed there before the declaration of war. This arsenal—you know where Maubeuge is situated!—points to agreements which Great Britain had made with France, and to which Belgium was also party. These agreements are before the whole world today, for the chain of evidence is complete and the treacherous plot of Great Britain is revealed. She has encouraged and pledged the Belgians against us, and therefore it is she who must answer for all the misery which has been visited upon that poor country. Had it been our responsibility, not a single hair of a Belgian's head should have been harmed. If, then, the Belgian wrongs like those of Serbia are only the flimsiest pretexts for Great Britain's declaration of war against us, there remains, unfortunately, no other reason for this declaration of war save the intention of your statesmen either to destroy us or so to weaken us that Great Britain will rule supreme on the seas and in all distant parts of the world. This intention you personally deny and thus far I must take your word for it. But do you deny it also for your Government? That you cannot do, for the facts have been brought to light; when Great Britain determined to join the coalition of Russia with France, which is ruled by Russia, when it put aside all the differences that stood between her and Russia, when it set upon us not only the hordes of Russia but the scrupulous Japanese, "the yellow peril," and called upon all Europe, when it also sunk in the ocean its duties to European culture—for all of that there is but one explanation: England believes that the hour for our destruction has struck. Why does she wish to destroy us? Because she will not endure our power, our zeal, our perfection of growth! There is no other explanation!

Lifting Humanity

We and Great Britain in alliance with America were able in peaceful co-operation to lift humanity to a higher plane, and to lead the world in peace, allowing to each his rights. We Germans, now know no, and have never known any, higher ideal than this. In order to realize this ideal the German Kaiser and the German people have made many sacrifices in the past 43 years. In proportion to the development of our strength, we should be able to lay claim to more territory than we now possess in the world. But we have never attempted to force this claim. We held that the strength of our nation should be in its zeal and in the peaceful fruits of that zeal. Great Britain has begrudged us that; she has been jealous of our powers, jealous of our fleet, jealous of our industries and our commerce, and jealousy is the root of all evil. Jealousy it is which has driven Great Britain into the most fearful war which history knows and the end of which is unforeseen.

What course is open to you, gentlemen, once you are enlightened as to the policy of your country? In the name of our Christian culture, which your Government has frivolously placed in jeopardy, I can offer you but one counsel: To burden your consciences no longer with Serbia and Belgium, which you must protect, but to face about and stop your Government in its headlong course; it may not be too late. As far as we Germans are concerned, our way is clearly indicated, though not so our fate. Should we fall, which God and our strong arm prevent, then there sinks with us to its grave all the higher culture of our part of the world, whose defenders we were called to be; for neither with Russia nor against Russia will Great Britain be able longer to maintain that culture in Europe. Should we conquer—and victory is for us something more than mere hope—then shall we feel ourselves responsible, as formerly, for this culture, for the learning and the peace of Europe, and shall put from us any idea of setting up a hegemony in Europe. We shall stand by the one who, together in fraternal union with us, will create and maintain such a peaceful Europe.

For the continuation of your cordial attitude toward me I am personally grateful. I would not unnecessarily sever the bond which holds me to the upright Christians and the learning of your country, but at the present moment this bond has no value for me.

PROF. VON HARNACK

P.S.—It is in your power now to wage a battle which would be of honor to you. As a fourth great power arrayed against Germany, the lying international press has raised itself up, flooded the world with lies about our splendid and upright army, and slandered everything that is German. We have been almost entirely cut off from any possibility of protecting ourselves against this "beast of the pit." Do not believe the lies, and spread abroad the truth about us. We are today no different than Carlyle pictured us to you.

HARNACK

EDITORIAL AND REFERENCE NOTES

Lecture One

1. The "building" to which Rudolf Steiner refers here, and will refer constantly in these lectures, is what has come to be called the first Goetheanum. Unless otherwise indicated, this will be the building that is meant.

2. *lebendig teilzunehmen mit unserer Seele*

3. Steiner elaborates on this point later in the lecture.

4. A seven-year-old boy from the community had been trapped beneath an overturned wagon and died. Because it was already dark, and because the boy usually ran his errands via a different route, nobody realized this initially.

5. Giotto di Bondone (1266-1337), Florentine painter and architect of the early Renaissance. Among his most famous works are the fresco cycle in the Arena (Scrovegni) Chapel in Padua, the fresco cycle on the life of St. Francis in Assisi, and the *campanile* or bell tower next to the Florentine *Duomo.*

6. *Faust,* lines 354-359, trans. Walter Arndt

7. George Henry Lewes (1817-1878); Steiner is referring to his *Life of Goethe* (1855).

8. *Faust,* lines 243-244, trans. Walter Arndt

9. The complete title is *From My Life: Poetry and Truth*, 2 vols. (New York: Suhrkamp, 1987; rpt. Princeton: Princeton University Press, 1994).

10. "Times of Expectation," October 7, 1914, in CW 156; *Inner Reading and Inner Hearing & How to Achieve Existence in the World of Ideas* (Great Barrington, MA: SteinerBooks, 2008), pp. 63-84. The full title of this lecture in German, "Das Zeitalter Herman Grimms als Zeitalter der Erwartung," would translate literally as "The Age of Herman Grimm as an Age of Expectation."

11. CW 18; *The Riddles of Philosophy* (1973; rpt. [Great Barrington, MA:] SteinerBooks, 2009). Originally published in 1914, this compendious history of philosophy (627 pp. in the standard German edition) is one of the most important texts in which Rudolf Steiner worked out the idea that Owen Barfield has termed "the evolution of consciousness." As opposed to conventional intellectual history, in which a succession of different ideas are seen as inhabiting epistemological structures presumed to be constant, Steiner argued forcefully that the structure of human consciousness itself has changed, and that it is the evolution of the structure of consciousness itself that is the main driver of the succession of different paradigms or mentalities that are the object of conventional intellectual history.

12. Steiner is likely referring to the notion of an "evolution of consciousness" described in the previous note.

13. The passage Steiner quotes is on p. 238 of the English translation, in the "Introductory Remarks to the 1914 Edition" that preface volume two. Steiner's use of the conjunction *wenn* ("if, although") is unusual but entirely grammatical, so one can understand his annoyance that the editors were really trying to change his meaning rather than correct his German. The editors must have assumed an error because Steiner's syntax creates a conditional with indicative verbs in two different tenses ("If I think x, then I was justified") where one would expect either a hypothetical conditional in the subjunctive ("If I thought x, then I would be justified") or a simple assertion in the indicative beginning with *da* ("since, because, as") with both verbs in the same tense ("Because I think x, I am justified"). The English translation sides with the editors by translating *wenn* as an assertion ("As it is the philosophical conviction…"), but Steiner *insists* here on a construction that should be translated: "If it is the philosophical conviction of the author of this book …, then it was permissible to append this chapter to his account." Hence I have modified the text of CW 18 accordingly. The difference is subtle but real.

14. This happened, and it was indeed called the "Philosophisch-Anthroposophischer Verlag."

15. Herman F. Grimm (1828-1901), the son of the famous linguist and folklorist Wilhelm Grimm, wrote extensively on literature and the history of art. He was widely read in the later nineteenth century. Steiner came to know Herman Grimm well during the years he was editing Goethe's scientific works at the Goethe Archives in Weimar, and he mentions Grimm often with great affection. See e.g. Ch. 14 of Steiner's autobiography, *The Course of My Life* (Hudson, NY: Anthroposophic Press, 1951), pp. 146-159, in which Grimm is contrasted with the cold positivist who led the entire project, Wilhelm Scherer. The reference to Hera snoring is in Grimm's book *Homer's Iliad*, Book Two (Berlin: Hertz, 1890).

16. This and the following passages from *The Iliad* are taken from the outstanding translation by Robert Fagles (New York: Viking, 1990).

17. *anschauen*

18. CW 156; *Inner Reading and Inner Hearing* (see note 10 above).

19. *in … "Lebensepisoden"… erleben konnte*

20. *Verstandes- oder Gemütsseele*

21. Xenophon (430-354 BCE) was a student of Socrates who became a mercenary and a historian. His greatest work, a staple of Great Books courses, is the *Anabasis*, which chronicles the military expedition of Cyrus the Younger against his older brother, King Artaxerxes II of Persia.

22. Phidias (490-430 BCE), perhaps the greatest of the Greek sculptors. His monumental Zeus at Olympia was considered one of the Seven Wonders of the ancient world, and he also created the colossal statue of Athena that stood within the Parthenon.

23. *plastisch*, literally "sculptural," unlike the merely two-dimensional figures we know from historical documents.

24. "Lycurgus … (ca. 820-730 BCE) was the legendary lawgiver of Sparta, who

established the military-oriented reformation of Spartan society in accordance with the Oracle of Apollo at Delphi. All his reforms were directed towards the three Spartan virtues: equality (among citizens), military fitness, and austerity." "Lycurgus of Sparta," *Wikipedia*, 29 Oct. 2016. Web.) It is doubtful whether Lycurgus was an actual historical figure.

25. Solon (ca. 638-558 BCE) was the statesman, legislator, and poet whose constitutional reforms were crucial in founding Athenian democracy. Few of his actual writings survive, and there are few documents extant regarding him or the period during which he lived generally.

26. Alcibaides (ca. 450-404 BCE) is the handsome, eloquent Athenian general and statesman who appears in several of Plato's dialogues, notably in the *Symposium*. Having been raised in the household of Pericles, he became the friend and pupil of Socrates. Alcibaides was undeniably brilliant, but also notoriously ambitious and dissolute.

27. CW 4; *The Philosophy of Freedom: The Basis for a Modern World Conception: Some results of introspective observation following the methods of Natural Science*, trans. Michael Wilson (London: Rudolf Steiner Press, 1964). (Alternative English translations are available under the titles *The Philosophy of Spiritual Activity and Intuitive Thinking as a Spiritual Path*.) Although Steiner did not identify it explicitly as such, CW 4 has come to be viewed as one of the four "basic books" of anthroposophy.

28. CW 13; *An Outline of Esoteric Science*, trans. Catherine E. Creeger (Great Barrington, MA: SteinerBooks, 1997). An earlier translation by George Adams bore the title *Occult Science*. At the time of writing, Steiner was the head of the Theosophical Society in Germany, and the word *Geheimwissenschaft* in his title was meant to echo Blavatsky's tome, *The Secret Doctrine*. CW 13 is now considered one of the four "basic books" of anthroposophy.

29. Steiner means those who were going off to fight in the war.

30. Geist seiner Seele, wirkender Wächter
Deine Schwingen mögen bringen
Unserer Seelen bittende Liebe
Deiner Hut vertrautem Sphärenmenschen;
Daß mit Deiner Macht strahle
Der Seele, die sie liebend sucht.

Lecture Two

31. *universelle und damit auch vieldeutige Schriftzeichen*

32. *wie sich uns Handhaben ergeben*, a particularly strong and graphic metaphor

33. "The Mystery of Golgotha" is Steiner's favored term for all that is more conventionally referred to as the Incarnation, the Passion, and the Resurrection. Steiner's early book *Christianity as Mystical Fact* situates Christianity within the context of ancient mystery religions (not mysticism, which the title might seem to imply). In the same spirit, Steiner also refers to "the Easter Mystery."

34. Steiner uses this theosophical term to designate a major historical era he saw as having begun ca. 747 BCE, and ended ca. 1413 CE. He also terms it the Greco-Roman epoch and the "intellectual soul epoch." The name implies that Greece and Rome were the "vanguard" cultures during the period, i.e. the loci of innovation and progress. He sees other cultures such as those of ancient India, Persia, and Egypt having been the leaders during even earlier periods. Steiner's terminology is idiosyncratic here, but the underlying thoughts are commonplaces of intellectual history.

35. For an excellent short summary of Steiner's thinking on this topic, see the account of "original participation" in Owen Barfield, *Saving the Appearances: A Study in Idolatry* (London: Faber, 1957; rpt. Middletown, CT: Wesleyan UP, 1988).

36. "The fifth [Post-Atlantean] cultural epoch" is Rudolf Steiner's theosophical term for the current historical epoch, which began ca. 1413—i.e., with the Renaissance. He saw it lasting until approximately 3573. Steiner also refers to this period as "the consciousness soul epoch."

37. *die ägyptisch-babylonisch-chaldäischen Kulturepoche*, which Steiner also terms, and will discuss below as "the sentient soul epoch."

38. "Etheric body" is Steiner's early, theosophical term for the subtle body of supra-physical forces that sustains life. Later he would also refer to it variously as "the life body," or the "formative forces body," or (echoing Spinoza's distinction between *natura naturans* and *natura naturata*), the realm of "living working" as opposed to the physical realm of "finished work." Theodor Schwenk's *Sensitive Chaos: The Creation of Flowing Forms in Water and Air* (London: Rudolf Steiner Press, 1996) is a scientifically compelling and aesthetically beautiful exploration of these forces.

39. This is Steiner's early, theosophical term that corresponds generally to "soul" or "psyche." Like Freud and Jung, he sees it as internally differentiated and transformed by the activity of the higher faculty of the "ego" or "I."

40. *Grundimpuls*

41. *Zeichen*, literally "sign"

42. Here Steiner is referring to a stage in the very distant, prehistoric past. Steiner's view of human evolution is laid out chiefly in Ch. 4 of CW 13; *An Outline of Esoteric Science* (see note 28).

43. Steiner's actual blackboard drawings accompanying this cycle of lectures have not been preserved. (It was only later that he began drawing on black construction paper, which could be taken down afterward and archived.) The figures in this volume were reconstructed for the German edition from various audience members' surviving notes by Leonore Uhlig.

44. *Empfindungsseele*. Basically, the "sentient soul" is the lowest level of the human psyche, at which it is mostly determined by the perceptions arriving through the bodily senses. The *locus classicus* for this term from Rudolf Steiner's early theosophical psychology is Chapter 1 of CW 9; *Theosophy* (1904; many English editions are available).

45. *Gestalt*

46. *der alten künstlerischen Schriftzeichen*, literally "of the ancient alphabets." Steiner's comment here resonates strongly with the work of the seminal art historian Aby Warburg (1866-1929). Although Warburg was Steiner's contemporary, his major works were published in full only after both had died, in 1932. Warburg's collected works are now available in English as *The Renewal of Pagan Antiquity: Contributions to the Cultural History of the European Renaissance* (Los Angeles: Getty Research Institute, 1999). Apropos "the mysteries of ancient artistic iconographies," see the many publications that later emanated from the Warburg Institute, notably those of Frances Yates, and especially Edgar Wind's magisterial study *Pagan Mysteries of the Renaissance: An Exploration of the Philosophical and Mystical Sources of Iconography in Renaissance Art* (2nd edn.; Norton, 1968). On Warburg's unfinished, encyclopedic *Atlas of Images: Mnemosyne*, see Christopher D. Johnson, *Memory, Metaphor and Aby Warburg's Atlas of Images* (Ithaca: Cornell University Press, 2012), which ties Warburg to another important and closely related thinker, Hans Blumenberg.

47. *Zeichen*

48. *Wiederauferstehung*

49. On the revival of ancient astrology in the Renaissance, see Frances A. Yates's magisterial study *Giordano Bruno and the Hermetic Tradition* (1964; Chicago: University of Chicago Press, 1991) and her important essay "The Hermetic Tradition in Renaissance Science" in Charles S. Singleton, ed., *Art, Science, and History in the Renaissance* (Baltimore: Johns Hopkins University Press, 1967), pp. 255-274. See also the chapter "Philosophical Renewal from Italy" in Peter Whitfield's more recent study *Astrology: A History* (New York: Abrams, 2001), pp. 144-165.

50. *Hingegebensein an die äußere Welt*. See note 35 on *Saving the Appearances*.

51. The standard scholarly studies of Babylonian and Egyptian astronomy and astrology are Otto Neugebauer's *The Exact Sciences in Antiquity* (Providence: Brown University Press, 1957; New York: Dover, 1969) and his book *A History of Ancient Mathematical Astronomy* (1975; Springer, 2013). Steiner's own, more esoteric studies of astronomy are to be found in two key cycles of lectures: CW 323; *Interdisciplinary Astronomy* (forthcoming from SteinerBooks in a new translation by Frederick Amrine) and CW 136; *Spiritual Beings in the Heavenly Bodies and in the Kingdoms of Nature* (Great Barrington, MA: SteinerBooks, 2012).

52. *Volksgemeinschaften*

53. *gleichsam*

54. Compare Steiner's statement about Dante to Robert M. Durling, "Seneca, Plato, and the Microcosm" in Harold Bloom, ed., *Modern Critical Views: Dante* (New York: Chelsea House, 1986), pp. 113-131.

55. *verseelischen*, a neologism

56. See the classic study *Saturn and Melancholy* by Raymond Klibansky, Erwin Panofsky, and Fritz Saxl (Nelson, 1964).

57. These are the eras that Steiner previously designated as the third, fourth, and fifth epochs respectively.

58. *das Mutterland ... von allem Formhaften*

59. Tommaso Campanella, *La Città del Sole: Dialogo Poetico / The City of the Sun: A Poetical Dialogue*, ed. and trans. by Daniel J. Donna (Berkeley: University of California Press, 1981). Campanella (1568-1639) was one of the major intellectual lights of the Italian Renaissance. He was a poet, a philosopher, a theologian and a scientist.

60. Pierre Corneille (1606-1684) was a major dramatist and a contemporary of Racine and Molière. He has been called "the father of French tragedy," but *Œdipe* (1659) is not considered one of his major works.

61. Voltaire was the pen-name of François-Marie Arouet (1694-1778). Arguably the most important writer and thinker of the French Enlightenment, Voltaire was a literary figure, a historian, and a philosopher. He is known for his mordant wit and his bold attacks on religious dogma. Few would include his *Œdipe* (1718) among his most important works.

62. *das Völkergeschicke-Lenkende*, a powerful neologism

63. Gotthold Ephraim Lessing (1729-1781), a major dramatist, philosopher, and theologian of the generation preceding Goethe. Lessing was a fascinating figure who hardly fits the stereotype of "Enlightenment rationalist" so often foisted upon him. A posthumous report that he had been a closet Spinozist (tantamount to an atheist in the minds of many) started a huge controversy that involved many of the major writers of the day, Goethe included. Anthroposophists will be intrigued to learn that late in life (ca. 1780) Lessing argued that humans must necessarily have more than five senses, and that we seem to be restricted to five only because the other, higher senses have not yet evolved. Lessing also published a late treatise, *The Education of the Human Race* (1777-1780), in which he attempts to reconcile the tensions between the religion of the Old Testament, the New Testament, and "the Christianity of reason" (as he termed it) by invoking the idea of reincarnation. There is a good English translation of these and other essays, edited by H. B. Nisbet: Lessing, *Philosophical and Theological Writings* (Cambridge: Cambridge University Press, 2005).

64. The classic "unities" of time, place, and action in Greek tragedy are described in Aristotle's *Poetics*; neo-classical writers and theorists later made Aristotle's descriptions into *prescriptions*.

65. Molière was the stage name of Jean-Baptiste Poquelin (1622-1673); his comedies are indeed timeless classics.

66. *Komik an sich*, literally "comedy in itself." The term *an sich* echoes Kant's Ding an sich, conventionally translated "the thing in itself."

67. *The Mission of the Folk-Souls in Relation to Teutonic Mythology* (London: Rudolf Steiner Press, 2005). Steiner gave these lectures in June 1910 in Christiania (now Oslo), Norway.

68. The *Staufer* (who later came to be called the Hohenstaufen by analogy to the Prussian Hohenzollern family) were the great Swabian dynasty who ruled in the High Middle Ages (1138-1254). Three of the *Staufer* were crowned Holy Roman Emperor.

69. "The Guelphs and Ghibellines ... were factions supporting the Pope and the Holy Roman Emperor, respectively, in central and northern Italy. During the 12th and 13th centuries, the rivalry between these two parties was a particularly important aspect of the internal policy of medieval Italy. The struggle for power between the Papacy and the Holy Roman Empire had arisen with the Investiture Conflict, which began in 1075 and ended with the Concordat of Worms in 1122. The division between the Guelphs and Ghibellines in Italy, however, persisted until the 15th century." ("Guelphs and Ghibellines." *Wikipedia*, 26 Oct. 2016. Web.)

70. The greatest German painter of the Renaissance, Albrecht Dürer (1471-1528), and probably Hans Holbein the Elder (1460-1524) rather than his son Hans Holbein the Younger (1497-1543), since the elder Holbein was Dürer's contemporary and more of a pioneer.

71. Dürer made two visits to Italy, in 1494-1495 and 1505-1507.

72. Peter von Cornelius (1784-1867) and Johann Friedrich Overbeck (1789-1869) were German painters who spent many years in Rome (no less than 59, in the case of Overbeck) and gathered together a group that called itself the Nazarenes. They sought to imitate the styles of Raphael and other Italian painters.

73. *Glied*, literally "member"

74. *Vorstellung*. Translators' introductions or notes invariably comment on the difficulty of translating *vorstellen/Vorstellung* and a few other German philosophical and psychological terms such as Geist, Anschauung, and Gemüt. Tellingly, in the title of Schopenhauer's *magnum opus*, *Die Welt als Wille und Vorstellung*, the term has been rendered three different ways: initially as "Representation," but then more recently as "Idea" and "Presentation." Both Michael Wilson's translation of Steiner's *Philosophy of Freedom* and Owen Barfield's *Case for Anthroposophy* (1970; Barfield Press, 2010) begin their discussions by noting that the standard translation of this Kantian philosophical term is "representation." But then Wilson goes on to argue (rightly) that this is too technical a term for most contexts, and that "representation" has other, distracting meanings outside of philosophy, which led him to translate *Vorstellung* and its variants as "mental picture." Barfield chooses "representation," which is understandable given that the context is Steiner's discussion of Brentano's neo-Kantian treatise. The reasons why this term is so very difficult to translate are (1) that it encompasses many different kinds of mental acts; (2) it refuses any sharp distinction between subjective and objective; (3) it can refer to a faculty, the activity of a faculty, or the result of that activity; (4) it often has a distinctly visual quality, but it can also refer to abstract concepts; and (5) it straddles the conventional divide between philosophy and psychology.

75. Gottfried Wilhelm Leibniz (1646-1716) was an important mathematician and metaphysician; he is universally regarded as one of the very greatest thinkers of his era. Leibniz developed calculus independently of Newton, and Leibniz's notation is now standard. A consummate rationalist, Leibniz anticipated many important aspects of contemporary analytic philosophy. He was also among many other things an important theologian, diplomat, and historian. Although a native speaker of German, Leibniz wrote his most important philosophical texts in French.

76. The Italian Dominican philosopher, scientist, and theologian Giordano Bruno (1548-1600) was burned at the stake by the Catholic Church on February 17, 1600. See the classic study by Frances Yates, *Giordano Bruno and the Hermetic Tradition* (Chicago: University of Chicago Press, 1964).

77. *ins Mitteleuropäische übertragen*, a neologism that imagines "Central European" as a language

78. Lessing's *Hamburg Dramaturgy* is a large, loosely organized collection of theater reviews and other reflections on the state of the German theater composed from 1767-1769. Lessing's main concern in this key text within the history of aesthetics was to show that French Classicism had profoundly misunderstood Aristotle by reducing his subtle understanding of empathy to a set of abstract rules regarding the supposed "unities" of time, place, and action.

79. *das spirituelle Wesen*

80. i*n die Konfiguration der Wesenheiten*; the translation intentionally replicates the vagueness of the original

81. Steiner later revised this work, *Welt- und Lebensfragen im neunzehnten Jahrhundert* (S. Cronbach, 1901), and published it as the first volume of *The Riddles of Philosophy* (see note 11). The earlier version has not appeared within the official *Gesamtausgabe* [Complete Works], nor has it ever been translated into English.

82. Owen Barfield deploys Steiner's term "onlooker consciousness" often in his various writings on the evolution of consciousness.

83. Johann Wolfgang von Goethe, *Scientific Studies*, vol. 12 of the Suhrkamp Edition [in English], ed. and trans. Douglas Miller (New York: Suhrkamp Publishers, 1988).

84. Jacob Böhme (1575-1624) was a great and prolific Silesian mystic and theologian whose works are however also notoriously obscure. Böhme began writing his most important text, *Aurora*, twelve years after a powerful spiritual experience befell him in 1600. It is indicative that, although it was his first work, Aurora remained unfinished at his death.

85. *der Gang des naturgemäßen Werdens der Ich-Kultur…aufstrebt*

86. Here Steiner is referring to Ernst Haeckel (1834-1919), Darwin's main apologist in Germany, and himself a great biologist. Haeckel propounded the "Ontogenetic Law" that "ontogeny recapitulates phylogeny," meaning that an organism's development (ontogeny) mirrors the development of its ancestors thoughout evolution (phylogeny). Haeckel was also an accomplished artist,

whose drawings of natural forms are prized to this day, and a major philosopher. Steiner studied Haeckel intensively, and he credits Haeckel's ideas with having contributed greatly to his own spiritual discoveries. On a related note, Stephen J. Gould's early book, *Ontogeny and Phylogeny* (Cambridge, MA: Harvard University Press, 1977), became the foundation of evolutionary developmental biology as it is currently practiced by taking seriously Haeckel's long-dismissed notion that ontogeny recapitulates phylogeny. For a good, brief discussion, see: K. J. McNamara and M. L. McKinney, "Heterochrony, disparity and macroevolution," in *Macroevolution: Diversity, Disparity, Contingency: Essays in Honor of Stephen Jay Gould*, ed. E. Vrba and N. Eldredge (Lawrence, KS: The Paleontological Society, 2005), pp. 17-26.

87. *wie auf den urewigen Säulen der Urgesetze der Menschheit ruhend*

88. *mit dem empfindenden Verständnis unserer Seelen*

89. *dasjenige, was geschieht*; literally, "that which happens"

90. *Geheimnisse der Weltordnung*

91. *energische Friedenskultur*

92. See the account of the tensions among those working to build the first Goetheanum in John Kettle's Introduction.

93. In Steiner's recent lecture of October 7, 1914, included in CW 156. See note 10.

94. Eugen Kühnemann (1868-1946), a German philosopher and literary historian. The speech to which Steiner refers was published under the title "An die deutsche Jugend im Weltkriegsjahr 1914 [(Address) To the Youth of Germany in the Year of the World War, 1914] (Leipzig: Köhler, 1914).

Lecture Three

95. In his later social theory, Steiner distinguishes what he came to call the "spiritual-cultural" sphere from that of the state and of the economy. See especially GA 24; *The Renewal of the Social Organism* (Spring Valley, NY: Anthroposophic Press, 1985), and GA 23; *Towards Social Renewal: Rethinking the Basis of Society*, (London: Rudolf Steiner Press, 1999). Earlier translations of the latter text bore various titles: *The Threefold Commonwealth* (London: Anthroposophical Publishing Co., 1923); *The Threefold Social Order* (n.p.: Anthroposophic Press, 1966; rpt. 1972); *Towards Social Renewal* (London: Rudolf Steiner Press, 1977; rpt. 1992).

96. *Gefüge*

97. Johann Gottlieb Fichte (1762-1814), the great pioneer of the post-Kantian phase of German Idealism, and the ultimate source of philosophical Romanticism in all its forms. Fichte claimed he was rewriting the letter of Kant in the spirit of Kant. His philosophy is esoteric and introspective. Steiner's own philosophical works are much indebted to Fichte.

98. There are two recent English translations of this important text by Fichte: *Addresses to the German Nation*, ed. Gregory Moore (Cambridge: Cambridge

University Press, 2008) and *Addresses to the German Nation*, ed. and trans. Isaac Nakhimovsky, Béla Kapossy, and Keith Tribe (Indianapolis: Hackett, 2013). More than two of the fourteen addresses Fichte gave originally in 1807 struggle to define what is "German," but Steiner probably means addresses four and six, in which Fichte focuses respectively on the German language and the Reformation. During the time leading up to German unification in the 1860s, the *Addresses* were held up as a gospel of messianic nationalism, and the same happened again in 1914 when the cultural right wing sought ammunition against Germany's enemies. Steiner rightly resists these propagandistic misreadings of Fichte, and he soon would be joined by no less a figure than the first President of the Weimar Republic, Friedrich Ebert, who argued in 1919 that Fichte was the *antidote* to German nationalism. In his excellent introduction, Gregory Moore has characterized Fichte's thought in a way that sounds uncannily similar to the idea of architecture as peacework elaborated in Steiner's lectures: "The key to his thinking can be found in an illuminating passage from *The Characteristic of the Present Age:* the 'fatherland of the really educated Christian European' is 'in each age the European state which leads in culture.'" (p. xxii)

99. *Deutschheit*

100. See CW 272, *Anthroposophy in the Light of Goethe's* Faust (Great Barrington, MA: SteinerBooks, 2014) and CW 273, *Goethe's* Faust *in the Light of Anthroposophy* (Great Barrington, MA: SteinerBooks, 2016).

101. Lines 11936-11937, spoken by the Angels after Faust's death to bear his "immortal essence" off to heaven, as translated by Walter Arndt. Tellingly, these two lines appear within quotation marks in the text of *Faust*, to signify that the Angels are delivering a pronouncement from above.

102. Lines 11575-11576 from Faust's final speech, as translated by Walter Arndt. They are strong evidence that even in old age Faust continues to strive, and hence deserves to win his wager with Mephistopheles.

103. *das Zu-etwas-Hinstreben*, a neologism worthy of Heidegger

104. This sentence resounds with distinctly Nietzschean overtones.

105. An unmistakable echo of Hegel's famous evocation of *der sich bildende Geist* ["the self-forming/self-cultivating Spirit"] in the Preface to his *Phenomenology of Spirit* (1807): "Spirit is indeed never at rest but always engaged in moving forward. But just as the first breath drawn by a child after its long, quiet nourishment breaks the gradualness of merely quantitative growth – there is a qualitative leap, and the child is born – so likewise the Spirit in its formation [*der sich bildende Geist*] matures slowly and quietly into its new shape, dissolving bit by bit the structure of its previous world, whose tottering state is only hinted at by isolated symptoms." (G. W. F. Hegel, *Phenomenology of Spirit,* trans. A. V. Miller [Oxford University Press, 1977], p. 6).

106. Lines 358-359, near the beginning of Faust's opening monologue, as translated by Walter Arndt.

107. The caduceus (from two Greek words meaning "herald's staff") was borne by Hermes and his female counterpart, Iris, in Greek mythology. It was eventually carried by heralds generally. Hermes' caduceus consists of a short vertical rod climbed by twin, intertwining serpents, often surmounted by wings. Confusion with the "rod of Asclepius" (one snake, no wings) has led to misuse of the caduceus as a symbol of the medical profession.

108. *Boten*

109. The word "archetypal" has been interpolated for the sake of clarity. Mercury is of course the Roman name for the Greek god Hermes, whence our modern name for textual interpretation as such: hermeneutics.

110. *Kulturbotschaft*, a standard German word and quite a conventional concept within German intellectual history

111. The Carpathian or Slovak Germans (also called the Zips Germans) are a group of ethnic Germans who lived in a region that is currently part of Slovakia and the western Ukraine. *Siebenbürgen* is the German name for the region that is called Transylvania in English, now the central provinces of Romania. The German name refers to seven ethnically German "Saxon" cities that were founded between 1142 and 1200. The Banat is a region of Central Europe that is currently divided among three different nation-states: Romania, Serbia, and Hungary. Its historical capital is Timişoara. Steiner's mentor and friend, the Goethe scholar Karl Julius Schröer (1825-1900), was an important philologist and folklorist who had deeply researched the dialects and literary artifacts of these cultures. Steiner's knowledge of these regions and his genuine interest in them grew directly out of his collaborations with Schröer.

112. This lecture was given on December 29, 1889. The actual text does not exist, but stenographic entries in one of Steiner's notebooks that seem to be notes for this lecture were eventually deciphered and published in the supplementary *Beiträge zur Rudolf Steiner-Gesamtausgabe*, No. 61/62 (1978), pp. 5-16.

113. Steiner's conclusion is clear and explicit: The existence of such communities of German-speaking "exiles" is not an occasion for invoking ethnic nationalism, but rather proof that ethnic nationalism can and should be overcome in favor of "the human as such." Sadly, Steiner remained a voice crying in the wilderness in this regard.

114. J. W. von Goethe, *Verse Plays and Epic*, Collected Works, vol. 8 (Princeton UP, 1995).

115. Goethe began an epic poem on Achilles in 1799, but he never completed more than the first "book" of 591 lines.

116. *Art des Seins*

117. Letter to Horace Walpole, July 15, 1768

118. Letter of August 23, 1794

119. Herman Grimm quotes this poem in his discussion of Book Two of the *Iliad* (*Homer: Ilias, erster bis neunter Gesang* [Berlin: Hertz, 1890]).

120. Presumably Steiner is referring to the Carpathian Ruthenians.

121. This aside could appear confusing given that this paragraph otherwise argues for a shared Central European identity. Steiner is here referring, however, to the Polish Messianism discussed in the following paragraph.

122. Andrzej Towiański (1799-1878) was a Polish philosopher and theologian who claimed to have "experienced a vision in which the Holy Ghost and the Virgin Mary urged him to act as a messenger of the Apocalypse. The Poles ... were to play leading roles." His thinking influenced Adam Mickiewicz (1798-1855), Juliusz Słowacki (1809-1849), and other Polish Romantics (*Wikipedia*). Mickiewicz was arguably the greatest Polish writer; he was also a political activist and an ardent Polish nationalist. Like Mickiewicz, Słowacki is considered one of the "Three Bards" of Polish literature and a major figure in Polish Romanticism. He has been called "the father of modern Polish drama," and his works feature "elements of Slavic pagan traditions, Polish history, mysticism and orientalism" (*Wikipedia*). None of these three figures was included in *The Riddles of Philosophy*, which Steiner had just completed.

123. Steiner seems to mean that the traditional element of religion is as alien to innate Polish individualism as the elements of Russian culture that he will label inauthentic later in this same lecture.

124. *Völkerkonglomerat*

125. *als Gemeinschaftliches*

126. Cf. the famous lines in Chapter Seven of Heinrich Heine's satire *Germany: A Winter's Tale*, which translate literally:

> One sleeps very well and also dreams well
> In our feather beds.
> Here the German soul feels free
> From all earthly chains.
>
> It feels free and soars upward
> Into the highest reaches of heaven.
> O German soul, how proud is thy flight
> Within your nightly dreams!
>
> The French and Russians own the land,
> The British own the sea,
> But within the airy realm of dreams
> We have unchallenged hegemony.

127. *Träumerei*

128. The Hanseatic League was a powerful economic and military alliance of guilds and various political entities that stretched across the North Sea and the Baltic from Belgium to Estonia. It flourished from the 13th to the end of the 16th century, and then persisted in nominal form until the last remainder was formally disbanded in 1862.

129. *Völkerseelenglieder*, a strong neologism that conjoins two more familiar German words: *Volksseele* ["folk-soul"] and *Seelenglieder* ["psychological faculties"]. Steiner seems to want to capture in this single difficult word the complexity of the whole foregoing argument, in which historical epochs are mapped systematically to the structure of the human constitution.

130. This is the final chapter that Steiner discusses in Lecture One.

131. Henri Bergson (1859-1941) was a great and highly influential philosopher who was also awarded the Nobel Prize in Literature. Bergson attempted to defend the possibility of human free will by radically redefining the notions of time, causality, and thinking. His most important publications were *Time and Free Will* (1889), *Matter and Memory* (1896), *Creative Evolution* (1907), and *The Two Sources of Morality and Religion* (1932). Just as Steiner notes unacknowledged parallels between Bergson and Preuss, others wondered aloud whether Bergson might not have borrowed central ideas regarding thought as a stream of consciousness from William James without acknowledging the debt. (Bergson denied this, and James later considered Bergson a personal friend and ally.) Both Steiner and Bergson argued that sense-bound, discursive thinking is inherently unable to penetrate the fluid nature of reality; hence the task of the philosopher and the scientist is to reorient thinking towards the higher faculty of intuition. Both saw intuitive thinking as releasing us from bodily processes. Steiner views Bergson's turn towards self-consciousness as typical of modern philosophy generally, but he is disappointed by Bergson's shallow vitalism when it comes to the question of biological evolution. The greatest philosopher of the second half of the twentieth century, Gilles Deleuze, has written an important study of Bergson: *Bergsonism* (New York: Zone Books, 1991).

132. Émile Boutroux (1845-1921) was a French philosopher and historian who sought to reconcile science and theology. Steiner was drawn to him for his resistance to the paradigm of materialist reductionism that was then dominant. Biological organisms cannot be explained in terms of inorganic processes, Boutreux claimed, because they cannot account for a creative force that has supervened at higher levels of complexity. Higher levels of complexity can each be explained in turn only by a supervening creative force, which implies nested hierarchies reaching all the way up to God. In *The Riddles of Philosophy*, Steiner focuses on Boutroux' book *The Idea of Natural Law in Science and Philosophy* (1895). There Boutreux argues that human thinking is founded in itself, and hence a free expression of the human soul. Like Steiner, Boutreux argues that the value of science is not its claim to explain the world (which is dubious), but rather its role in fostering the pure thinking of a self-conscious human ego.

133. p. 423. Wilhelm Heinrich Preuss (1843-1909) was an obscure thinker whom Steiner discovered and promoted as the antithesis of Darwin. What drew Steiner to him was especially his theory that human nature is not the end-point but rather the beginning of evolution, and that the animal forms are "cast-offs" as it were from a gradually incarnating, ideal human archetype.

134. Wilhelm Wundt (1832-1920) was an important German philosopher

and scientist. A student of Hermann von Helmholtz, he is widely credited with having founded modern experimental psychology in 1879 by creating the first laboratory devoted to that subject exclusively. The co-founder and first President of the American Psychological Association, G. Stanley Hall, had studied with Wundt in Leipzig.

135. *"Der Ton macht die Musik,"* literally "the tone makes the music"

136. *so etwas Läppisches*

137. Wundt's demotion of Bergson from "Professor" to "Mr." would have been taken as a profound insult, as was surely intended.

138. *Chiromantie*

139. *die Strukturverhältnisse des Seelenlebens der Völker*

140. Although he never traveled there, Steiner felt a deep connection with Russian culture, married a Russian, and counted several important Russian avant-garde artists among his students, including notables such as Wassily Kandinsky and Andrei Bely.

141. *"Schlangenheit,"* a neologism

142. *das Gefaltete*

143. *ein Nicht-Fertiges*

144. Within Steiner's spiritual psychology, "spirit self" or "manas" is the name for a future state of consciousness within which the faculties of thinking, feeling, and willing as they currently exist will have been strengthened and reoriented away from the physical body toward the spirit through the activity of our self-conscious ego. Steiner sees this "transformed astral body" or "selfless self" as inherently altruistic. At present we see only glimmerings of it in highly developed individuals, he claimed, but several centuries hence it will have become a universal human consciousness.

145. Peter the Great (a.k.a. Peter I or Pyotr Alexeyevich) ruled Russia from 1682-1725. He sought to modernize Russia by importing ideas from the West.

146. Vladimir Sergeyevich Solovyov (1853-1900) was a major Russian theologian, philosopher, and literary figure who influenced profoundly the Symbolist movement in the early 20th century as well as the religious philosophies of major theologians such as Nicolas Berdyaev, Sergey Bulgakov, and Pavel Florensky. Steiner also refers to him often in many different contexts. Solovyov became a close friend of Fyodor Dostoyevsky, and it has been claimed that Solovyov was an important model for both Ivan and Alyosha in *The Brothers Karamazov*. Many editions of Solovyov's writings are now available in English, notable among them *War, Progress, and the End of History* (Hudson, New York: Lindisfarne Books, 1990); *Lectures on Divine Humanity* (Hudson, New York: Lindisfarne Books, 1995); and *The Meaning of Love*, intro. Owen Barfield (Hudson, New York: Lindisfarne Books, 1995).

147. The translations to which Steiner refers were all published between 1909 and June 1914. The important translations by Harriet von Vacano (1862-1949) were published under her pseudonym "Harry Köhler." She joined the

Theosophical Society in 1904, and was both an esoteric student of Steiner's and a close friend of his wife. At Steiner's behest, the anthroposophical publishing house *Die Kommenden* later issued her multi-volume German translation of Solovyov's works in 1921-1922, beginning with *The Spiritual Foundations of Life*. Steiner himself wrote the preface to that edition.

148. *durch die fühlende Seele*

149. *Untertönen*

150. Steiner seems to have taken this quote, as well as the following references to Bakunin, Dostoevsky, and Gorky, from Dmitry Merezhkovsky's book [Dmitri Mereschkowski,] *Der Anmarsch des Pöbels* [*The Advance of the Mob*] (Munich: Piper, 1907): Voltaire's witticism is quoted on p. 17, for example. Merezhkovsky (1866-1941) was a major literary figure and religious thinker who co-founded the Symbolist movement, of which many Russian émigrés in Steiner's immediate circle were also members. He attended Steiner's lectures in Paris from May 25-June 14, 1906, a synopsis of which has been published in English as *An Esoteric Cosmology: Evolution, Christ & Modern Spirituality* (Great Barrington, MA: SteinerBooks, 2008). Steiner framed these lectures with the Symbolists in mind, and planned to give them in Russia, but was prevented by the political situation, so instead he held them in Paris, which was home to many exiled Russian artists and intellectuals. It is important to understand that, although Steiner uses many of Merezhkovsky's references, the conclusions he draws from them are very different, and Steiner's political views are diametrically opposed. On Steiner's employment of Merezhkovsky's book, see further notes below.

151. Mikhail Bakunin (1814-1876), a Russian political revolutionary and philosopher of anarchism. Merezhkovsky's book begins with an eponymous essay criticizing both Bakunin and the great Russian socialist Alexander Herzen (1812-1870). See Isaiah Berlin's classic study *Russian Thinkers* (Penguin, 2008) on the nineteenth-century Russian intelligentsia generally and on Herzen (Berlin's hero) and Bakunin in particular.

152. The quote is from Bakunin's late work *God and the State*, written in 1871 and published in 1882.

153. These are exactly his words in the German translation Steiner had read.

154. What follows is a close and accurate paraphrase of the original.

155. *sich auf sein Wesen erst vorbereitet*

156. "The Devil. Ivan Fyodorovich's Nightmare," Book 11, Chapter 9 of Fyodor Dostoevsky, *The Brothers Karamazov*, trans. Richard Pevear and Larissa Volokhonsky (1880; New York: Farrar, Strauss and Giroux, 1990), pp. 634-650. Steiner probably has in mind the passage paraphrased on p. 17 of Merezhkovsky's *Anmarsch:* "In my opinion, there is no need to destroy anything, one need only destroy the idea of God in mankind, that's where the business should start! One should begin with that, with that – oh, blind men, of no understanding! Once mankind has renounced God, one and all (and I believe that this period, analogous to the geological periods, will come), then the entire old world view will fall of itself, without anthropophagy, and, above all, the entire former

morality, and everything will be new" (*The Brothers Karamazov*, pp. 648-649).

157. Maxim Gorky, the pseudonym of Alexei Maximovich Peshkov (1868-1936), a Russian writer and political activist who became the leading literary proponent of Socialist Realism during the Stalinist period. His pen-name is the Russian adjective meaning "bitter."

158. Quoted in the second essay of Merezhkovsky's book, "Chekhov and Gorky," p. 70f.

159. The quote is from Gorky's play "Night Asylum" (1902). Although Merezhkovsky discusses this drama in his book, I was unable to find any reference to these particular lines.

160. *daß die weitere Evolution ad absurdum gehen müßte*. Steiner is likely referring to the outbreak of World War One.

161. *jenes Schützende*

162. *im Unterbewußtsein*

163. Friedrich von Bernhardi (1849-1930) was a Prussian general and military historian who had been a hero of the Franco-Prussian War. Bernhardi's bellicose and nationalistic bestseller was published in 1912.

164. Rudolf Steiner spoke often about the dual nature of evil, ascribing its source to supersensible beings he calls Lucifer and Ahriman. For an excellent discussion of Steiner's ideas as applied to Goethe's *Faust*, see Alan P. Cottrell, *Goethe's View of Evil and the Search for a New Image of Man in our Time* (Edinburgh: Floris Press, 1982). Mephistopheles in Goethe's Faust exhibits traits of both beings by turns, and Steiner was critical of Goethe for having conflated them. Lucifer and Ahriman also appear as characters in Steiner's own expressionist *Mystery Dramas* (1910-1913): see GA 14, Rudolf Steiner, *Four Mystery Dramas*, trans. Ruth and Hans Pusch (Great Barrington, MA: SteinerBooks, 2014). Lucifer might be termed the "red devil," who tempts humans to sin on the side of *superbia*: pride, anger, egotism, erotic passions, etc. "Ahriman" is a traditional name for a black demon, beginning with the Zoroastrian figure Angra Mainyu, opponent of the Sun God Ahura Mazda. Ahriman's temptations are those of *acedia*: laziness, greed, and denial of the Spirit generally. Steiner argues that the assaults of these beings are providential: only by overcoming their resistance and holding them in proper balance can humanity become inwardly strong enough to develop genuine freedom, knowledge, and love.

165. Italian, literally "deadly leap," originally a daring somersault. Steiner is using the term sarcastically to describe a wild leap in Bernhardi's argument.

166. See John Kettle's Introduction.

167. Steiner makes up a new word, *Großigkeiten* [literally "bignesses"] by analogy to the standard German word for "details," *Kleinigkeiten* [literally "smallnesses"].

168. Steiner is referring to the soul of the murdered Archduke. Again, see John Kettle's Introduction.

169. *Kraftmittelpunkt*

170. Cf. the study by Christopher Clark, *The Sleepwalkers: How Europe Went to*

War in 1914 (New York: HarperCollins, 2012) which confirms already in its title Steiner's assertion that the main actors in this tragedy stumbled into war in a state of diminished consciousness.

171. Sent by eleven British theologians, dated August 27, 1914. The full text of the letter and an English translation of Harnack's reply is to be found in the Appendix. Harnack's speech to which the British theologians replied was given on August 11, 1914 in Berlin.

172. *phrasenhaft*

173. J. W. von Goethe, *The Sayings of Goethe* (1819; London: Duckworth, 1996). Steiner chose this quote as the epigraph to the Articles of the Constitution of the Anthroposophical Society that he wrote in 1912. The German original [*Die Weisheit ist nur in der Wahrheit*] is more forceful in its brevity and alliteration.

174. *eine Umschreibung*, literally "a paraphrase"

Lecture Four

175. *empfindungsgemäß*

176. *nicht in verstandesmäßiger, symbolischer Weise*

177. *Summe*, literally a "sum"

178. *das dynamische, das kraftliche [Element]*; in order to underscore the importance of this point, Steiner coins a new word, *kraftlich*, as opposed to the standard adjective *kräftig* ("forceful," "forcible").

179. Regarding the origin, nature, and significance of the elementary spirits, see CW 136; *Spiritual Beings in the Heavenly Bodies and in the Kingdoms of Nature* (Great Barrington, MA: SteinerBooks, 2012), especially the lectures of April 3 and 4, 1912.

180. CW 156; *Inner Reading and Inner Hearing & How to Achieve Existence in the World of Ideas* (Great Barrington, MA: SteinerBooks, 2008). See especially the lecture of October 6, 1914, pp. 87-100.

181. *das Erlebnis des Erfühlens der Welt*. The German prefix *er-* usually implies repeated action to the end of internalizing something, as e.g. in the difference between *lernen* ["to learn"] and *erlernen* ["to master a subject"]. Hence "feeling our way into."

182. *himmelwärts hat*. This unidiomatic phrase has been translated literally.

183. *in seinem Befühlen der Welt*

184. *Fühlsphäre*, a strong neologism

185. *hinauszutasten in die Welt*

186. *Dann müssen wir aber sinngemäß die andere Richtung verfolgen*

187. *des Fortschreitens*, "moving forward" both literally and figuratively

188. *die aus der Willenssphäre kommende Willensbeschränktheit*

189. "The Anthroposophical Society is to be an association of people whose will it is to nurture the life of the soul, both in the individual and in human society, on the basis of a true knowledge of the spiritual world."

190. *sowohl in als auch an unserem Bau*

191. *das Abschließende...das Deckende...das Überdeckende.* Here and in the following paragraphs Steiner shuns abstract nouns and reaches instead for various grammatical forms of participles, many of them neologisms. The result is grammatical and stylistic awkwardness in the original that surely is intended as a way of highlighting enlivened inner activity.

192. *tatsächlich mitmachen*

193. *dieses Von-unten-nach-oben-Gehen,* a strong neologism

194. *ein gewisses Etwas*

195. "Maya" is a theosophical term that Steiner uses frequently. It is a contraction of the Sanskrit terms *maha* [great], a [not or non-, like "alpha privative" in Ancient Greek; cf. "apolitical"], and *ya* [being]; hence, "maya" means literally "the great non-being." It is illusory because it seems to exist, but ultimately does not.

196. The traditional poet-patriarchs of the Vedic religion. Steiner refers to them frequently as the founders of the Ancient Indian cultural epoch, and he asserts that they were real, historical personages rather than mythic figures.

197. *das Werden*

198. *der da liegt im Weltenwerden*

199. For a full discussion of this very difficult topic, see "The Foundation Stone Meditation in Eurythmy (*An Esoteric Contemplation*), Ch. 4 of Sergei Prokofieff's book *May Human Beings Hear It!: The Mystery of the Christmas Conference* (Forest Row: Temple Lodge, 2004), pp. 261-305.

200. *geschaut*

201. *was in der Menschheitsevolution vorhanden ist*

202. *im Völkerwerden*

203. *Entwickelung ihrer selbst*

204. *eine Kunstvorstellung.* See the discussion of the term *Vorstellung* in the note in Lecture Two.

205. *Vorstellungen*

206. *Vorstellungen*

207. *ein inbrünstiges Gefühl*

208. *wenn wir symbolisch uns etwa sagen*

Lecture Five

209. *Übergangsimpulse*

210. *Kräfte,* which could mean either "forces" or "faculties" or both.

211. *in dem, was malerisch anzustreben ist,* literally: "in that which is to be striven for in painting." *Das Malerische* is the German name for a fundamental concept introduced by the great art historian Heinrich Wölfflin, which is usually translated as "the painterly" (as opposed to *das Zeichnerische,* "the linear"), and many of Steiner's pronouncements on painting (in this lecture and elsewhere)

call for the subordination of line to color. But Wölfflin's study that made these categories so famous would not be published for another year (*Principles of Art History* [*Kunstgeschichtliche Grundbegriffe*], 1915), so Steiner cannot be referring to it. Nevertheless, it is both possible and intriguing to translate this phrase as "what we must strive to accomplish in a painterly way"—especially in light of the following paragraph, which clearly anticipates Wölfflin's famous distinction. Wölfflin was Swiss, and he had both studied and taught for many years at the nearby University of Basel: did he hear, or hear of, these lectures by Steiner?

212. See Heinrich Wölfflin, "Linear and Painterly," Ch. 1 of *Principles of Art History: The Problem of the Development of Style in Later Art* (New York: Dover, 1950), pp. 18-72, esp. pp. 18-23.

213. *dasjenige, was in den Wesen innerlich formhaft veranlagt ist*

214. *ein Bild des Formhaften*

215. *was in einem Wesen*

216. *das Innere, Wesenhafte*

217. See, for example, Monet's impressionistic haystacks, which first puzzled and then captured the imagination of Steiner's student Wassily Kandinsky when he encountered them at an exhibition in Moscow in 1896. This encounter changed his idea of painting fundamentally, and strengthened Kandinsky's resolve to become a painter.

218. Steiner seems to be getting at a fundamental distinction between Impressionism and what was just emerging as Expressionism in the visual arts.

219. CW 156; see note 180 above.

220. Steiner works out this important idea more fully in at least three other places besides CW 156: a lecture Steiner gave at the International Philosophical Congress in Bologna on April 8, 1911 (published as *Seeing with the Soul* [Spring Valley, NY: Mercury Press]); the last chapter of his *Riddles of Philosophy* (see above); and in CW 326; *The Origins of Natural Science*, intro. Owen Barfield (Spring Valley, NY: Anthroposophic Press, 1985).

221. *vorstellen*. See the discussion of this term in the note in Lecture Two.

222. The Ancient Greeks, for example, viewed the rainbow as a bridge traversed by a divine messenger. Their word for "rainbow," *iris*, was also the name of a goddess, who was the female counterpart of Hermes.

223. CW 286; *Architecture as a Synthesis of the Arts* (London: Rudolf Steiner Press, 1999). See especially the lecture of July 26, 1914, "The Creative World of Colour," pp. 132-150.

224. *das Schöpferische der Farben*

225. *sich wesenhaft ausleben*

226. *daß also die Form das Werk der Farbe ist.* These words are are a reminiscent those spoken by Strader as he marvels at Johannes Thomasius' painted portrait of Capesius in Scene Eight of Steiner's first Mystery Drama, *The Portal of Initiation.* It is a riddle and a challenge to the skeptical scientist how the artist's use of color can capture spiritual realities. Strader's long, anguished response to Thomasius'

portrait is a perfect little inverse manifesto on the new painting, worthy of Kandinsky, and worth quoting at length:

> My friend's soul power shines
> out of these eyes, though they are merely painted.
> The scholar's thoughtfulness
> lives on this brow;
> the innate warmness of his words
> streams from each color tone
> with which your brush
> has solved this riddle.
> O all these colors,—they are only surface,
> and yet they're not.
> It is as if they're only visible
> to make themselves invisible to me.
> These forms,
> emerging as the colors' interplay,
> speak of the spirit's weaving.
> Indeed they speak of much
> which they themselves are not.

Rudolf Steiner, *Four Mystery Dramas* (Great Barrington, MA: SteinerBooks, 2014), p. 130.

227. *mitleben*, "participate" in the high Platonic and anthropological sense. See Owen Barfield, *Saving the Appearances: A Study in Idolatry* (London: Faber, 1957; rpt. 2nd edition. Middletown, Connecticut: Wesleyan University Press, 1988).

228. *Farbenerfassen*

229. *Formerfassung*

230. There are important connection between Steiner's descriptions of a new kind of painting here and the experiments of groups such as The Blue Rider in Munich, who were deeply influenced by Steiner's teachings. See e.g. the classic study by Sixten Ringbom, *Sounding Cosmos: A Study in the Spiritualism of Kandinsky and the Genesis of Abstract Painting*, Acta academiae Åboensis, ser. A, v. 38, No. 2 (Åbo [Turku]: Åbo Akademi, 1970), and also his articles "Kandinsky und das Okkulte" and "Die Steiner-Annotationen Kandinskys" in Armin Zweite, ed., *Kandinsky und München: Begegnungen und Wandlungen 1896-1914* (München: Prestel-Verlag, 1982), pp. 85-105. The hero of Steiner's four Mystery Dramas, performed in Munich from 1910-1913, is a painter named Johannes Thomasius. His monologue at the beginning of Scene Three of the second drama, *The Soul's Probation*, is an eloquent evocation of the spirit that animated the "new painting" in Munich right before the war.

231. There is a lacuna in the stenogram at this point. The plot Steiner describes is that of Grimms' fairy tale "The White Serpent."

232. Cf. Wassily Kandinsky, *Concerning the Spiritual in Art* (New York: Dover, 1977).

233. *zusammengedrängt*

234. *das Wahrzeichen*. Again we see that it is actually not symbolism but rather allegorical transpositions of concepts that Steiner opposes in his aesthetics.

235. *Vorstellungen*

236. Homer, *Iliad*, Book One, lines 423-425: "Only yesterday Zeus went off to the Ocean River / to feast with the Ethiopians, loyal, lordly men, / and all the gods went with him. But in twelve days / the Father returns to Olympus."

237. *äußerlich physisch*: Another possible translation of these puzzling adverbs would be to take them as modifying "be" rather than "discover." Indeed, an earlier translation of this lecture that has circulated in typescript rendered this sentence: "For in the outer world there will be physical men who need to discover Goethe in this way." That interpretation makes less sense, I think, even though it is closer to the syntax of the original.

238. *fortschreitende Richtung*

239. Here Steiner alludes to the all-important scene "Dark Gallery" in Part Two of Goethe's *Faust*, where Faust travels to the spiritual realm of the archetypes of creativity, imagined as "the Mothers." When Faust asks Mephistopheles for directions to this underworld, the devil answers cryptically: "Well then, sink down! Or I might call it: soar! / It's all one and the same" [lines 6275-6276]. In seeming to mislead Faust, Mephisto actually reveals a profound mystery: Faust's goal lies entirely outside of space and time. Cf. Heraclitus 69: "The way up and the way down are one and the same."

240. *Vorstellung*

241. *Vorstellung*

242. *Vorstellungen*

243. *Reihe von Vorstellungen*

244. *diese Vorstellungen zusammenhalten*

245. [*auf den Flächen*] interpolated by the editors of the German edition

246. As was the case now that war had broken out.

247. *seine Hauptanlage*, a pun in the original German that turns on the double meanings of *Haupt* (both "main" in the sense of "most important" and the anatomical "head") and *Anlage* (both "structure" and "predisposition" or "aptness"). Thus *seine Hauptanlage* means both "its main structural basis" and something like "its propensity for headness."

248. This term from Steiner's highly esoteric cosmogony refers not to the physical star at the center of our Solar System, but rather to an earlier evolutionary stage or "incarnation" of the entire cosmos. "Old Sun" was preceded by "Old Saturn," and followed by "Old Moon." (Cf. the names of the days of the week, which are a holdover from a lapsed clairvoyance: Saturn-day, Sun-day, Moon-day.) Future states of the cosmos Steiner terms "Jupiter," "Venus," and "Vulcan." The *locus classicus* is Ch. 4 of Steiner's book *Outline of Esoteric Science*.

249. *Kopf*, a metonymy for "mind" here

250. Cf. CW 323; *Interdisciplinary Astronomy: Third Scientific Course* (forthcoming from SteinerBooks), passim.

251. *Vorstellung*

252. Steiner seems to be playing on 1 Corinthians 15:13-14: "But if there be no resurrection of the dead, then is Christ not risen: and if Christ be not risen, then is our preaching vain, and your faith is also vain." The Greek word translated as "resurrection," *anastasis*, means literally "standing up."

253. *Kopfgehirn*

254. CW 156, the cycle of lectures to which Steiner has already referred in Lectures One, Two, and Four. See especially the lecture of October 6, 1914, "Inner Mobility of Thought," pp. 47-62.

255. *nicht gut möglich*

256. *Urkunden*

257. *herunterholen*, literally "pull down from above"

258. See Owen Barfield, *Poetic Diction: A Study in Meaning* (1928; 2nd revised edition Middletown, CT: Wesleyan University Press, 1984), Owen Barfield, *History in English Words* (1953; Great Barrington, MA: Lindisfarne Press, 1985), and Owen Barfield, "The Meaning of 'Literal'," in *The Rediscovery of Meaning and Other Essays* (Middletown, CT: Wesleyan University Press, 1977), pp. 32-43.

259. Here Steiner is referring to "eurythmy," the art of movement he inaugurated in 1912. Eurythmy has three different aspects: artistic, pedagogical, and curative. Although they are no substitute for seeing or, better, practicing eurythmy, Steiner gave numerous lectures describing it. See e.g. CW 277a, *Eurythmy: Its Birth and Development*, translation Alan Stott (Anastasi, 2002); CW 278, originally issued under the title *Eurythmy as Visible Music* (London: Rudolf Steiner Press, 1977), and more recently by Alan Stott under the title *Eurythmy as Visible Singing*, 2 vols., 4th edition. (Stourbridge: The Anderida Music Trust, 2013); and CW 279, *Eurythmy as Visible Speech* (London: Rudolf Steiner Press, 1984). In addition, Steiner gave hundreds of short addresses by way of introducing eurythmy performances, see CW 277c; *The Early History of Eurythmy: Notebook Entries, Addresses, Rehearsals, Programs, Introductions to Performances, and a Chronology, 1913–1924* (Great Barrington, MA: SteinerBooks, 2015).

260. *vorstellen*

261. "Volapük...is a constructed language, created in 1879–1880 by Johann Martin Schleyer, a Roman Catholic priest in Baden, Germany. Schleyer felt that God had told him in a dream to create an international language. Volapük conventions took place in 1884 (Friedrichshafen), 1887 (Munich) and 1889 (Paris). The first two conventions used German, and the last conference used only Volapük. In 1889, there were an estimated 283 clubs, 25 periodicals in or about Volapük, and 316 textbooks in 25 languages; at that time the language claimed nearly a million adherents. Volapük was largely displaced in the late 19th and early 20th centuries by Esperanto and Ido." (*Wikipedia*)

262. Esperanto is an artificially constructed international language, inaugurated by L. L. Zamenhof's book *Unua Libro* published in 1887. One of Zamenhof's main intentions was to help foster world peace. The first World Congress of

Esperanto was held in France in 1905. The progress of the language has remained very restricted to this day.

263. *unorganisch,* literally "inorganically"

264. *ein rechtes Schweben im Wolkenkuckucksheim,* literally "a downright hovering in cloud-cuckoo-land"

265. Matthew 24:35, Mark 13:31, and Luke 21:33

RUDOLF STEINER'S COLLECTED WORKS

The German Edition of Rudolf Steiner's Collected Works (the *Gesamtausgabe* [GA] published by Rudolf Steiner Verlag, Dornach, Switzerland) presently runs to 354 titles, organized either by type of work (written or spoken), chronology, audience (public or other), or subject (education, art, etc.). For ease of comparison, the Collected Works in English [CW] follows the German organization. A complete listing of the CWs follows with *literal translations* of the German titles. Other than in the case of the books published in his lifetime, titles were rarely given by Rudolf Steiner himself, and were often provided by the editors of the German editions. The titles in English are not necessarily the same as the German; and, indeed, over the past seventy-five years have frequently been different, with the same book sometimes appearing under different titles.

For ease of identification and to avoid confusion, we suggest that readers looking for a title should do so by CW number. Because the work of creating the Collected Works of Rudolf Steiner is an ongoing process, with new titles being published every year, we have not indicated in this listing which books are presently available. To find out what titles in the Collected Works are currently in print, please check our website at www.steinerbooks.org, or write to: SteinerBooks; 610 Main Street, Great Barrington, MA 01230.

A. Written Work

I. Writings 1884–1925

CW 1 Goethe: Natural-Scientific Writings, Introduction, with Footnotes and Explanations in the text by Rudolf Steiner

CW 2 Outlines of an Epistemology of the Goethean World View, with Special Consideration of Schiller

CW 3 Truth and Science

CW 4 The Philosophy of Freedom

CW 4a Documents to "The Philosophy of Freedom"

CW 5 Friedrich Nietzsche, A Fighter against His Own Time

CW 6 Goethe's Worldview

CW 6a *[Now in CW 30]*

CW 7 Mysticism at the Dawn of Modern Spiritual Life and Its Relationship with Modern Worldviews

CW 8 Christianity as Mystical Fact and the Mysteries of Antiquity

CW 9 Theosophy: An Introduction into Supersensible World Knowledge and Human Purpose

CW 10 How Does One Attain Knowledge of Higher Worlds?

CW 11 From the Akasha-Chronicle

CW 12 Levels of Higher Knowledge

CW 13 Occult Science in Outline

CW 14 Four Mystery Dramas

CW 15	The Spiritual Guidance of the Individual and Humanity
CW 16	A Way to Human Self-Knowledge: Eight Meditations
CW 17	The Threshold of the Spiritual World. Aphoristic Comments
CW 18	The Riddles of Philosophy in Their History, Presented as an Outline
CW 19	*[Contained in CW 24]*
CW 20	The Riddles of the Human Being: Articulated and Unarticulated in the Thinking, Views and Opinions of a Series of German and Austrian Personalities
CW 21	The Riddles of the Soul
CW 22	Goethe's Spiritual Nature and Its Revelation in "Faust" and through the "Fairy Tale of the Snake and the Lily"
CW 23	The Central Points of the Social Question in the Necessities of Life in the Present and the Future
CW 24	Essays Concerning the Threefold Division of the Social Organism and the Period 1915-1921
CW 25	Cosmology, Religion and Philosophy
CW 26	Anthroposophical Leading Thoughts
CW 27	Fundamentals for Expansion of the Art of Healing according to Spiritual-Scientific Insights
CW 28	The Course of My Life

II. Collected Essays

CW 29	Collected Essays on Dramaturgy, 1889-1900
CW 30	Methodical Foundations of Anthroposophy: Collected Essays on Philosophy, Natural Science, Aesthetics and Psychology, 1884-1901
CW 31	Collected Essays on Culture and Current Events, 1887-1901
CW 32	Collected Essays on Literature, 1884-1902
CW 33	Biographies and Biographical Sketches, 1894-1905
CW 34	Lucifer-Gnosis: Foundational Essays on Anthroposophy and Reports from the Periodicals "Lucifer" and "Lucifer-Gnosis," 1903-1908
CW 35	Philosophy and Anthroposophy: Collected Essays, 1904-1923
CW 36	The Goetheanum-Idea in the Middle of the Cultural Crisis of the Present: Collected Essays from the Periodical "Das Goetheanum," 1921-1925
CW 37	*[Now in CWs 251 and 260a]*

III. Publications from the Literary Estate

CW 38	Letters, Vol. 1: 1881-1890
CW 39	Letters, Vol. 2: 1890-1925
CW 40	Truth-Wrought Words
CW 40a	Sayings, Poems and Mantras; Supplementary Volume
CW 42	*[Now in CWs 264-266]*

CW 43 Stage Adaptations
CW 44 On the Four Mystery Dramas. Sketches, Fragments and Paralipomena on the Four Mystery Dramas
CW 45 Anthropsophy: A Fragment from the Year 1910

B. Lectures

I. Public Lectures

CW 51 On Philosophy, History and Literature
CW 52 Spiritual Teachings Concerning the Soul and Observation of the World
CW 53 The Origin and Goal of the Human Being
CW 54 The Riddles of the World and Anthroposophy
CW 55 Knowledge of the Supersensible in Our Times and Its Meaning for Life Today
CW 56 Knowledge of the Soul and of the Spirit
CW 57 Where and How Does One Find the Spirit?
CW 58 The Metamorphoses of the Soul Life. Paths of Soul Experiences: Part One
CW 59 The Metamorphoses of the Soul Life. Paths of Soul Experiences: Part Two
CW 60 The Answers of Spiritual Science to the Biggest Questions of Existence
CW 61 Human History in the Light of Spiritual Research
CW 62 Results of Spiritual Research
CW 63 Spiritual Science as a Treasure for Life
CW 64 Out of Destiny-Burdened Times
CW 65 Out of Central European Spiritual Life
CW 66 Spirit and Matter, Life and Death
CW 67 The Eternal in the Human Soul. Immortality and Freedom
CW 68 Public lectures in various cities, 1906-1918
CW 69 Public lectures in various cities, 1906-1918
CW 70 Public lectures in various cities, 1906-1918
CW 71 Public lectures in various cities, 1906-1918
CW 72 Freedom – Immortality – Social Life
CW 73 The Supplementing of the Modern Sciences through Anthroposophy
CW 73a Specialized Fields of Knowledge and Anthroposophy
CW 74 The Philosophy of Thomas Aquinas
CW 75 Public lectures in various cities, 1906-1918
CW 76 The Fructifying Effect of Anthroposophy on Specialized Fields
CW 77a The Task of Anthroposophy in Relation to Science and Life: The Darmstadt College Course
CW 77b Art and Anthroposophy. The Goetheanum-Impulse
CW 78 Anthroposophy, Its Roots of Knowledge and Fruits for Life

CW 79 The Reality of the Higher Worlds
CW 80 Public lectures in various cities, 1922
CW 81 Renewal-Impulses for Culture and Science–Berlin College Course
CW 82 So that the Human Being Can Become a Complete Human Being
CW 83 Western and Eastern World-Contrast. Paths to Understanding It through Anthroposophy
CW 84 What Did the Goetheanum Intend and What Should Anthroposophy Do?

II. Lectures to the Members of the Anthroposophical Society

CW 88 Concerning the Astral World and Devachan
CW 89 Consciousness – Life – Form. Fundamental Principles of a Spiritual-Scientific Cosmology
CW 90 Participant Notes from the Lectures during the Years 1903-1905
CW 91 Participant Notes from the Lectures during the Years 1903-1905
CW 92 The Occult Truths of Ancient Myths and Sagas
CW 93 The Temple Legend and the Golden Legend
CW 93a Fundamentals of Esotericism
CW 94 Cosmogony. Popular Occultism. The Gospel of John. The Theosophy in the Gospel of John
CW 95 At the Gates of Theosophy
CW 96 Origin-Impulses of Spiritual Science. Christian Esotericism in the Light of New Spirit-Knowledge
CW 97 The Christian Mystery
CW 98 Nature Beings and Spirit Beings – Their Effects in Our Visible World
CW 99 The Theosophy of the Rosicrucians
CW 100 Human Development and Christ-Knowledge
CW 101 Myths and Legends. Occult Signs and Symbols
CW 102 The Working into Human Beings by Spiritual Beings
CW 103 The Gospel of John
CW 104 The Apocalypse of John
CW 104a From the Picture-Script of the Apocalypse of John
CW 105 Universe, Earth, the Human Being: Their Being and Development, as well as Their Reflection in the Connection between Egyptian Mythology and Modern Culture
CW 106 Egyptian Myths and Mysteries in Relation to the Active Spiritual Forces of the Present
CW 107 Spiritual-Scientific Knowledge of the Human Being
CW 108 Answering the Questions of Life and the World through Anthroposophy
CW 109 The Principle of Spiritual Economy in Connection with the Question of Reincarnation. An Aspect of the Spiritual Guidance of Humanity

CW 110 The Spiritual Hierarchies and Their Reflection in the Physical World. Zodiac, Planets and Cosmos
CW 111 *[Contained in CW 109]*
CW 112 The Gospel of John in Relation to the Three Other Gospels, Especially the Gospel of Luke
CW 113 The Orient in the Light of the Occident. The Children of Lucifer and the Brothers of Christ
CW 114 The Gospel of Luke
CW 115 Anthroposophy – Psychosophy – Pneumatosophy
CW 116 The Christ-Impulse and the Development of "I"- Consciousness
CW 117 The Deeper Secrets of the Development of Humanity in Light of the Gospels
CW 118 The Event of the Christ-Appearance in the Etheric World
CW 119 Macrocosm and Microcosm. The Large World and the Small World. Soul-Questions, Life-Questions, Spirit-Questions
CW 120 The Revelation of Karma
CW 121 The Mission of Individual Folk-Souls in Connection with Germanic-Nordic Mythology
CW 122 The Secrets of the Biblical Creation-Story. The Six-Day Work in the First Book of Moses
CW 123 The Gospel of Matthew
CW 124 Excursus in the Area of the Gospel of Mark
CW 125 Paths and Goals of the Spiritual Human Being. Life Questions in the Light of Spiritual Science
CW 126 Occult History. Esoteric Observations of the Karmic Relationships of Personalities and Events of World History
CW 127 The Mission of the New Spiritual Revelation. The Christ-Event as the Middle-Point of Earth Evolution
CW 128 An Occult Physiology
CW 129 Wonders of the World, Trials of the Soul, and Revelations of the Spirit
CW 130 Esoteric Christianity and the Spiritual Guidance of Humanity
CW 131 From Jesus to Christ
CW 132 Evolution from the View Point of the Truth
CW 133 The Earthly and the Cosmic Human Being
CW 134 The World of the Senses and the World of the Spirit
CW 135 Reincarnation and Karma and their Meaning for the Culture of the Present
CW 136 The Spiritual Beings in Celestial Bodies and the Realms of Nature
CW 137 The Human Being in the Light of Occultism, Theosophy and Philosophy
CW 138 On Initiation. On Eternity and the Passing Moment. On the Light of the Spirit and the Darkness of Life
CW 139 The Gospel of Mark

CW 140	Occult Investigation into the Life between Death and New Birth. The Living Interaction between Life and Death
CW 141	Life between Death and New Birth in Relationship to Cosmic Facts
CW 142	The Bhagavad Gita and the Letters of Paul
CW 143	Experiences of the Supersensible. Three Paths of the Soul to Christ
CW 144	The Mysteries of the East and of Christianity
CW 145	What Significance Does Occult Development of the Human Being Have for the Sheaths – Physical Body, Etheric Body, Astral Body, and Self?
CW 146	The Occult Foundations of the Bhagavad Gita
CW 147	The Secrets of the Threshold
CW 148	Out of Research in the Akasha: The Fifth Gospel
CW 149	Christ and the Spiritual World. Concerning the Search for the Holy Grail
CW 150	The World of the Spirit and Its Extension into Physical Existence; The Influence of the Dead in the World of the Living
CW 151	Human Thought and Cosmic Thought
CW 152	Preliminary Stages to the Mystery of Golgotha
CW 153	The Inner Being of the Human Being and Life Between Death and New Birth
CW 154	How does One Gain an Understanding of the Spiritual World? The Flowing in of Spiritual Impulses from out of the World of the Deceased
CW 155	Christ and the Human Soul. Concerning the Meaning of Life. Theosophical Morality. Anthroposophy and Christianity
CW 156	Occult Reading and Occult Hearing
CW 157	Human Destinies and the Destiny of Peoples
CW 157a	The Formation of Destiny and the Life after Death
CW 158	The Connection Between the Human Being and the Elemental World. Kalevala – Olaf Asteson – The Russian People – The World as the Result of the Influences of Equilibrium
CW 159	The Mystery of Death. The Nature and Significance of Middle Europe and the European Folk Spirits
CW 160	*[In CW 159]*
CW 161	Paths of Spiritual Knowledge and the Renewal of the Artistic Worldview
CW 162	Questions of Art and Life in Light of Spiritual Science
CW 163	Coincidence, Necessity and Providence. Imaginative Knowledge and the Processes after Death
CW 164	The Value of Thinking for a Knowledge That Satisfies the Human Being. The Relationship of Spiritual Science to Natural Science
CW 165	The Spiritual Unification of Humanity through the Christ-Impulse

CW 166 Necessity and Freedom in World Events and in Human Action
CW 167 The Present and the Past in the Human Spirit
CW 168 The Connection between the Living and the Dead
CW 169 World-being and Selfhood
CW 170 The Riddle of the Human Being. The Spiritual Background of Human History. Cosmic and Human History, Vol. 1
CW 171 Inner Development-Impulses of Humanity. Goethe and the Crisis of the 19th Century. Cosmic and Human History, Vol. 2
CW 172 The Karma of the Vocation of the Human Being in Connection with Goethe's Life. Cosmic and Human History, Vol. 3
CW 173 Contemporary-Historical Considerations: The Karma of Untruthfulness, Part One. Cosmic and Human History, Vol. 4
CW 174 Contemporary-Historical Considerations: The Karma of Untruthfulness, Part Two. Cosmic and Human History, Vol. 5
CW 174a Middle Europe between East and West. Cosmic and Human History, Vol. 6
CW 174b The Spiritual Background of the First World War. Cosmic and Human History, Vol. 7
CW 175 Building Stones for an Understanding of the Mystery of Golgotha. Cosmic and Human Metamorphoses
CW 176 Truths of Evolution of the Individual and Humanity. The Karma of Materialism
CW 177 The Spiritual Background of the Outer World. The Fall of the Spirits of Darkness. Spiritual Beings and Their Effects, Vol. 1
CW 178 Individual Spiritual Beings and their Influence in the Soul of the Human Being. Spiritual Beings and their Effects, Vol. 2
CW 179 Spiritual Beings and Their Effects. Historical Necessity and Freedom. The Influences on Destiny from out of the World of the Dead. Spiritual Beings and Their Effects, Vol. 3
CW 180 Mystery Truths and Christmas Impulses. Ancient Myths and their Meaning. Spiritual Beings and Their Effects, Vol. 4
CW 181 Earthly Death and Cosmic Life. Anthroposophical Gifts for Life. Necessities of Consciousness for the Present and the Future.
CW 182 Death as Transformation of Life
CW 183 The Science of the Development of the Human Being
CW 184 The Polarity of Duration and Development in Human Life. The Cosmic Pre-History of Humanity
CW 185 Historical Symptomology
CW 185a Historical-Developmental Foundations for Forming a Social Judgment
CW 186 The Fundamental Social Demands of Our Time–In Changed Situations
CW 187 How Can Humanity Find the Christ Again? The Threefold Shadow-Existence of our Time and the New Christ-Light

CW 188 Goetheanism, a Transformation-Impulse and Resurrection-Thought. Science of the Human Being and Science of Sociology
CW 189 The Social Question as a Question of Consciousness. The Spiritual Background of the Social Question, Vol. 1
CW 190 Impulses of the Past and the Future in Social Occurrences. The Spiritual Background of the Social Question, Vol. 2
CW 191 Social Understanding from Spiritual-Scientific Cognition. The Spiritual Background of the Social Question, Vol. 3
CW 192 Spiritual-Scientific Treatment of Social and Pedagogical Questions
CW 193 The Inner Aspect of the Social Riddle. Luciferic Past and Ahrimanic Future
CW 194 The Mission of Michael. The Revelation of the Actual Mysteries of the Human Being
CW 195 Cosmic New Year and the New Year Idea
CW 196 Spiritual and Social Transformations in the Development of Humanity
CW 197 Polarities in the Development of Humanity: West and East Materialism and Mysticism Knowledge and Belief
CW 198 Healing Factors for the Social Organism
CW 199 Spiritual Science as Knowledge of the Foundational Impulses of Social Formation
CW 200 The New Spirituality and the Christ-Experience of the 20th Century
CW 201 The Correspondences Between Microcosm and Macrocosm. The Human Being – A Hieroglyph of the Universe. The Human Being in Relationship with the Cosmos: 1
CW 202 The Bridge between the World-Spirituality and the Physical Aspect of the Human Being. The Search for the New Isis, the Divine Sophia. The Human Being in Relationship with the Cosmos: 2
CW 203 The Responsibility of Human Beings for the Development of the World through their Spiritual Connection with the Planet Earth and the World of the Stars. The Human Being in Relationship with the Cosmos: 3
CW 204 Perspectives of the Development of Humanity. The Materialistic Knowledge-Impulse and the Task of Anthroposophy. The Human Being in Relationship with the Cosmos: 4
CW 205 Human Development, World-Soul, and World-Spirit. Part One: The Human Being as a Being of Body and Soul in Relationship to the World. The Human Being in Relationship with the Cosmos: 5
CW 206 Human Development, World-Soul, and World-Spirit. Part Two: The Human Being as a Spiritual Being in the Process of Historical Development. The Human Being in Relationship with the Cosmos: 6

CW 207 Anthroposophy as Cosmosophy. Part One: Characteristic Features of the Human Being in the Earthly and the Cosmic Realms. The Human Being in Relationship with the Cosmos: 7
CW 208 Anthroposophy as Cosmosophy. Part Two: The Forming of the Human Being as the Result of Cosmic Influence. The Human Being in Relationship with the Cosmos: 8
CW 209 Nordic and Central European Spiritual Impulses. The Festival of the Appearance of Christ. The Human Being in Relationship with the Cosmos: 9
CW 210 Old and New Methods of Initiation. Drama and Poetry in the Change of Consciousness in the Modern Age
CW 211 The Sun Mystery and the Mystery of Death and Resurrection. Exoteric and Esoteric Christianity
CW 212 Human Soul Life and Spiritual Striving in Connection with World and Earth Development
CW 213 Human Questions and World Answers
CW 214 The Mystery of the Trinity: The Human Being in Relationship with the Spiritual World in the Course of Time
CW 215 Philosophy, Cosmology, and Religion in Anthroposophy
CW 216 The Fundamental Impulses of the World-Historical Development of Humanity
CW 217 Spiritually Active Forces in the Coexistence of the Older and Younger Generations. Pedagogical Course for Youth
CW 217a Youth's Cognitive Task
CW 218 Spiritual Connections in the Forming of the Human Organism
CW 219 The Relationship of the World of the Stars to the Human Being, and of the Human Being to the World of the Stars. The Spiritual Communion of Humanity
CW 220 Living Knowledge of Nature. Intellectual Fall and Spiritual Redemption
CW 221 Earth-Knowing and Heaven-Insight
CW 222 The Imparting of Impulses to World-Historical Events through Spiritual Powers
CW 223 The Cycle of the Year as Breathing Process of the Earth and the Four Great Festival-Seasons. Anthroposophy and the Human Heart (*Gemüt*)
CW 224 The Human Soul and its Connection with Divine-Spiritual Individualities. The Internalization of the Festivals of the Year
CW 225 Three Perspectives of Anthroposophy. Cultural Phenomena observed from a Spiritual-Scientific Perspective
CW 226 Human Being, Human Destiny, and World Development
CW 227 Initiation-Knowledge
CW 228 Science of Initiation and Knowledge of the Stars. The Human Being in the Past, the Present, and the Future from the Viewpoint of the Development of Consciousness

CW 229	The Experiencing of the Course of the Year in Four Cosmic Imaginations
CW 230	The Human Being as Harmony of the Creative, Building, and Formative World-Word
CW 231	The Supersensible Human Being, Understood Anthroposophically
CW 232	The Forming of the Mysteries
CW 233	World History Illuminated by Anthroposophy and as the Foundation for Knowledge of the Human Spirit
CW 233a	Mystery Sites of the Middle Ages: Rosicrucianism and the Modern Initiation-Principle. The Festival of Easter as Part of the History of the Mysteries of Humanity
CW 234	Anthroposophy. A Summary after 21 Years
CW 235	Esoteric Observations of Karmic Relationships in 6 Volumes, Vol. 1
CW 236	Esoteric Observations of Karmic Relationships in 6 Volumes, Vol. 2
CW 237	Esoteric Observations of Karmic Relationships in 6 Volumes, Vol. 3: The Karmic Relationships of the Anthroposophical Movement
CW 238	Esoteric Observations of Karmic Relationships in 6 Volumes, Vol. 4: The Spiritual Life of the Present in Relationship to the Anthroposophical Movement
CW 239	Esoteric Observations of Karmic Relationships in 6 Volumes, Vol. 5
CW 240	Esoteric Observations of Karmic Relationships in 6 Volumes, Vol. 6
CW 243	The Consciousness of the Initiate
CW 245	Instructions for an Esoteric Schooling
CW 250	The Building-Up of the Anthroposophical Society. From the Beginning to the Outbreak of the First World War
CW 251	The History of the Goetheanum Building-Association
CW 252	Life in the Anthroposophical Society from the First World War to the Burning of the First Goetheanum
CW 253	The Problems of Living Together in the Anthroposophical Society. On the Dornach Crisis of 1915. With Highlights on Swedenborg's Clairvoyance, the Views of Freudian Psychoanalysts, and the Concept of Love in Relation to Mysticism
CW 254	The Occult Movement in the 19th Century and Its Relationship to World Culture. Significant Points from the Exoteric Cultural Life around the Middle of the 19th Century
CW 255	Rudolf Steiner during the First World War
CW 255a	Anthroposophy and the Reformation of Society. On the History of the Threefold Movement
CW 255b	Anthroposophy and Its Opponents, 1919-1921
CW 256	How Can the Anthroposophical Movement Be Financed?
CW 256a	Futurum, Inc. / International Laboratories, Inc.
CW 256b	The Coming Day, Inc.
CW 257	Anthroposophical Community-Building

CW 258 The History of and Conditions for the Anthroposophical Movement in Relationship to the Anthroposophical Society. A Stimulus to Self-Contemplation
CW 259 The Year of Destiny 1923 in the History of the Anthroposophical Society. From the Burning of the Goetheanum to the Christmas Conference
CW 260 The Christmas Conference for the Founding of the General Anthroposophical Society
CW 260a The Constitution of the General Anthroposophical Society and the School for Spiritual Science. The Rebuilding of the Goetheanum
CW 261 Our Dead. Addresses, Words of Remembrance, and Meditative Verses, 1906-1924
CW 262 Rudolf Steiner and Marie Steiner-von Sivers: Correspondence and Documents, 1901-1925
CW 263/1 Rudolf Steiner and Edith Maryon: Correspondence: Letters, Verses, Sketches, 1912-1924
CW 264 On the History and the Contents of the First Section of the Esoteric School from 1904 to 1914. Letters, Newsletters, Documents, Lectures
CW 265 On the History and from the Contents of the Ritual-Knowledge Section of the Esoteric School from 1904 to 1914. Documents, and Lectures from the Years 1906 to 1914, as Well as on New Approaches to Ritual-Knowledge Work in the Years 1921-1924
CW 266/1 From the Contents of the Esoteric Lessons. Volume 1: 1904-1909. Notes from Memory of Participants. Meditation texts from the notes of Rudolf Steiner
CW 266/2 From the Contents of the Esoteric Lessons. Volume 2: 1910-1912. Notes from Memory of Participants
CW 266/3 From the Contents of the Esoteric Lessons. Volume 3: 1913, 1914 and 1920-1923. Notes from Memory of Participants. Meditation texts from the notes of Rudolf Steiner
CW 267 Soul-Exercises: Vol. 1: Exercises with Word and Image Meditations for the Methodological Development of Higher Powers of Knowledge, 1904-1924
CW 268 Soul-Exercises: Vol. 2: Mantric Verses, 1903-1925
CW 269 Ritual Texts for the Celebration of the Free Christian Religious Instruction. The Collected Verses for Teachers and Students of the Waldorf School
CW 270 Esoteric Instructions for the First Class of the School for Spiritual Science at the Goetheanum 1924, 4 Volumes

III. Lectures and Courses on Specific Realms of Life

Lectures on Art

CW 271 Art and Knowledge of Art. Foundations of a New Aesthetic
CW 272 Spiritual-Scientific Commentary on Goethe's "Faust" in Two

Volumes. Vol. 1: Faust, the Striving Human Being
CW 273 Spiritual-Scientific Commentary on Goethe's "Faust" in Two Volumes. Vol. 2: The Faust-Problem
CW 274 Addresses for the Christmas Plays from the Old Folk Traditions
CW 275 Art in the Light of Mystery Wisdom
CW 276 The Artistic in Its Mission in the World. The Genius of Language. The World of Self-Revealing Radiant Appearances – Anthroposophy and Art. Anthroposophy and Poetry
CW 277 Eurythmy. The Revelation of the Speaking Soul
CW 277a The Origin and Development of Eurythmy
CW 278 Eurythmy as Visible Song
CW 279 Eurythmy as Visible Speech
CW 280 The Method and Nature of Speech Formation
CW 281 The Art of Recitation and Declamation
CW 282 Speech Formation and Dramatic Art
CW 283 The Nature of Things Musical and the Experience of Tone in the Human Being
CW 284/285 Images of Occult Seals and Pillars. The Munich Congress of Whitsun 1907 and Its Consequences
CW 286 Paths to a New Style of Architecture. "And the Building Becomes Human"
CW 287 The Building at Dornach as a Symbol of Historical Becoming and an Artistic Transformation Impulse
CW 288 Style-Forms in the Living Organic
CW 289 The Building-Idea of the Goetheanum: Lectures with Slides from the Years 1920-1921
CW 290 The Building-Idea of the Goetheanum: Lectures with Slides from the Years 1920-1921
CW 291 The Nature of Colors
CW 291a Knowledge of Colors. Supplementary Volume to "The Nature of Colors"
CW 292 Art History as Image of Inner Spiritual Impulses

<u>*Lectures on Education*</u>

CW 293 General Knowledge of the Human Being as the Foundation of Pedagogy
CW 294 The Art of Education, Methodology and Didactics
CW 295 The Art of Education: Seminar Discussions and Lectures on Lesson Planning
CW 296 The Question of Education as a Social Question
CW 297 The Idea and Practice of the Waldorf School
CW 297a Education for Life: Self-Education and the Practice of Pedagogy
CW 298 Rudolf Steiner in the Waldorf School
CW 299 Spiritual-Scientific Observations on Speech
CW 300a Conferences with the Teachers of the Free Waldorf School in

	Stuttgart, 1919 to 1924, in 3 Volumes, Vol. 1
CW 300b	Conferences with the Teachers of the Free Waldorf School in Stuttgart, 1919 to 1924, in 3 Volumes, Vol. 2
CW 300c	Conferences with the Teachers of the Free Waldorf School in Stuttgart, 1919 to 1924, in 3 Volumes, Vol. 3
CW 301	The Renewal of Pedagogical-Didactical Art through Spiritual Science
CW 302	Knowledge of the Human Being and the Forming of Class Lessons
CW 302a	Education and Teaching from a Knowledge of the Human Being
CW 303	The Healthy Development of the Human Being
CW 304	Methods of Education and Teaching Based on Anthroposophy
CW 304a	Anthroposophical Knowledge of the Human Being and Pedagogy
CW 305	The Soul-Spiritual Foundational Forces of the Art of Education. Spiritual Values in Education and Social Life
CW 306	Pedagogical Praxis from the Viewpoint of a Spiritual-Scientific Knowledge of the Human Being. The Education of the Child and Young Human Beings
CW 307	The Spiritual Life of the Present and Education
CW 308	The Method of Teaching and the Life-Requirements for Teaching
CW 309	Anthroposophical Pedagogy and Its Prerequisites
CW 310	The Pedagogical Value of a Knowledge of the Human Being and the Cultural Value of Pedagogy
CW 311	The Art of Education from an Understanding of the Being of Humanity

Lectures on Medicine

CW 312	Spiritual Science and Medicine
CW 313	Spiritual-Scientific Viewpoints on Therapy
CW 314	Physiology and Therapy Based on Spiritual Science
CW 315	Curative Eurythmy
CW 316	Meditative Observations and Instructions for a Deepening of the Art of Healing
CW 317	The Curative Education Course
CW 318	The Working Together of Doctors and Pastors
CW 319	Anthroposophical Knowledge of the Human Being and Medicine

Lectures on Natural Science

CW 320	Spiritual-Scientific Impulses for the Development of Physics 1: The First Natural-Scientific Course: Light, Color, Tone, Mass, Electricity, Magnetism
CW 321	Spiritual-Scientific Impulses for the Development of Physics 2: The Second Natural-Scientific Course: Warmth at the Border of Positive and Negative Materiality
CW 322	The Borders of the Knowledge of Nature

CW 323 The Relationship of the various Natural-Scientific Fields to Astronomy
CW 324 Nature Observation, Mathematics, and Scientific Experimentation and Results from the Viewpoint of Anthroposophy
CW 324a The Fourth Dimension in Mathematics and Reality
CW 325 Natural Science and the World-Historical Development of Humanity since Ancient Times
CW 326 The Moment of the Coming Into Being of Natural Science in World History and Its Development Since Then
CW 327 Spiritual-Scientific Foundations for Success in Farming. The Agricultural Course

Lectures on Social Life and the Threefold Arrangement of the Social Organism

CW 328 The Social Question
CW 329 The Liberation of the Human Being as the Foundation for a New Social Form
CW 330 The Renewal of the Social Organism
CW 331 Work-Council and Socialization
CW 332 The Alliance for Threefolding and the Total Reform of Society. The Council on Culture and the Liberation of the Spiritual Life
CW 332a The Social Future
CW 333 Freedom of Thought and Social Forces
CW 334 From the Unified State to the Threefold Social Organism
CW 335 The Crisis of the Present and the Path to Healthy Thinking
CW 336 The Great Questions of the Times and Anthroposophical Spiritual Knowledge
CW 337a Social Ideas, Social Reality, Social Practice, Vol. 1: Question-and-Answer Evenings and Study Evenings of the Alliance for the Threefold Social Organism in Stuttgart, 1919-1920
CW 337b Social Ideas, Social Realities, Social Practice, Vol. 2: Discussion Evenings of the Swiss Alliance for the Threefold Social Organism
CW 338 How Does One Work on Behalf of the Impulse for the Threefold Social Organism?
CW 339 Anthroposophy, Threefold Social Organism, and the Art of Public Speaking
CW 340 The National-Economics Course. The Tasks of a New Science of Economics, Volume 1
CW 341 The National-Economics Seminar. The Tasks of a New Science of Economics, Volume 2

Lectures and Courses on Christian Religious Work

CW 342 Lectures and Courses on Christian Religious Work, Vol. 1: Anthroposophical Foundations for a Renewed Christian Religious Working

CW 343 Lectures and Courses on Christian Religious Work, Vol. 2: Spiritual Knowledge – Religious Feeling – Cultic Doing
CW 344 Lectures and Courses on Christian Religious Work, Vol. 3: Lectures at the Founding of the Christian Community
CW 345 Lectures and Courses on Christian Religious Work, Vol. 4: Concerning the Nature of the Working Word
CW 346 Lectures and Courses on Christian Religious Work, Vol. 5: The Apocalypse and the Work of the Priest

Lectures for Workers at the Goetheanum

CW 347 The Knowledge of the Nature of the Human Being According to Body, Soul and Spirit. On Earlier Conditions of the Earth
CW 348 On Health and Illness. Foundations of a Spiritual-Scientific Doctrine of the Senses
CW 349 On the Life of the Human Being and of the Earth. On the Nature of Christianity
CW 350 Rhythms in the Cosmos and in the Human Being. How Does One Come To See the Spiritual World?
CW 351 The Human Being and the World. The Influence of the Spirit in Nature. On the Nature of Bees
CW 352 Nature and the Human Being Observed Spiritual-Scientifically
CW 353 The History of Humanity and the World-Views of the Folk Cultures
CW 354 The Creation of the World and the Human Being. Life on Earth and the Influence of the Stars

SIGNIFICANT EVENTS IN THE LIFE OF RUDOLF STEINER

1829: June 23: birth of Johann Steiner (1829-1910)—Rudolf Steiner's father—in Geras, Lower Austria.

1834: May 8: birth of Franciska Blie (1834-1918)—Rudolf Steiner's mother—in Horn, Lower Austria. "My father and mother were both children of the glorious Lower Austrian forest district north of the Danube."

1860: May 16: marriage of Johann Steiner and Franciska Blie.

1861: February 25: birth of *Rudolf Joseph Lorenz Steiner* in Kraljevec, Croatia, near the border with Hungary, where Johann Steiner works as a telegrapher for the South Austria Railroad. Rudolf Steiner is baptized two days later, February 27, the date usually given as his birthday.

1862: Summer: the family moves to Mödling, Lower Austria.

1863: The family moves to Pottschach, Lower Austria, near the Styrian border, where Johann Steiner becomes stationmaster. "The view stretched to the mountains...majestic peaks in the distance and the sweet charm of nature in the immediate surroundings."

1864: November 15: birth of Rudolf Steiner's sister, Leopoldine (d. November 1, 1927). She will become a seamstress and live with her parents for the rest of her life.

1866: July 28: birth of Rudolf Steiner's deaf-mute brother, Gustav (d. May 1, 1941).

1867: Rudolf Steiner enters the village school. Following a disagreement between his father and the schoolmaster, whose wife falsely accused the boy of causing a commotion, Rudolf Steiner is taken out of school and taught at home.

1868: A critical experience. Unknown to the family, an aunt dies in a distant town. Sitting in the station waiting room, Rudolf Steiner sees her "form," which speaks to him, asking for help. "Beginning with this experience, a new soul life began in the boy, one in which not only the outer trees and mountains spoke to him, but also the worlds that lay behind them. From this moment on, the boy began to live with the spirits of nature...."

1869: The family moves to the peaceful, rural village of Neudörfl, near Wiener-Neustadt in present-day Austria. Rudolf Steiner attends the village school. Because of the "unorthodoxy" of his writing and spelling, he has to do "extra lessons."

1870: Through a book lent to him by his tutor, he discovers geometry: "To grasp something purely in the spirit brought me inner happiness. I know that I first learned happiness through geometry." The same tutor allows him to draw, while other students still struggle with their reading and writing. "An artistic element" thus enters his education.

1871: Though his parents are not religious, Rudolf Steiner becomes a "church child," a favorite of the priest, who was "an exceptional character." "Up to the age of ten or eleven, among those I came to know, he was far and away the most significant." Among other things, he introduces Steiner to Copernican, heliocentric cosmology. As an altar boy, Rudolf Steiner serves at Masses, funerals, and Corpus Christi processions. At year's end, after an incident in which he escapes a thrashing, his father forbids him to go to church.

1872: Rudolf Steiner transfers to grammar school in Wiener-Neustadt, a five-mile walk from home, which must be done in all weathers.

1873-75: Through his teachers and on his own, Rudolf Steiner has many wonderful experiences with science and mathematics. Outside school, he teaches himself analytic geometry, trigonometry, differential equations, and calculus.

1876: Rudolf Steiner begins tutoring other students. He learns bookbinding from his father. He also teaches himself stenography.

1877: Rudolf Steiner discovers Kant's *Critique of Pure Reason*, which he reads and rereads. He also discovers and reads von Rotteck's *World History.*

1878: He studies extensively in contemporary psychology and philosophy.

1879: Rudolf Steiner graduates from high school with honors. His father is transferred to Inzersdorf, near Vienna. He uses his first visit to Vienna "to purchase a great number of philosophy books"—Kant, Fichte, Schelling, and Hegel, as well as numerous histories of philosophy. His aim: to find a path from the "I" to nature.

October 1879-1883: Rudolf Steiner attends the Technical College in Vienna—to study mathematics, chemistry, physics, mineralogy, botany, zoology, biology, geology, and mechanics—with a scholarship. He also attends lectures in history and literature, while avidly reading philosophy on his own. His two favorite professors are Karl Julius Schröer (German language and literature) and Edmund Reitlinger (physics). He also audits lectures by Robert Zimmerman on aesthetics and Franz Brentano on philosophy. During this year he begins his friendship with Moritz Zitter (1861-1921), who will help support him financially when he is in Berlin.

1880: Rudolf Steiner attends lectures on Schiller and Goethe by Karl Julius Schröer, who becomes his mentor. Also "through a remarkable combination of circumstances," he meets Felix Koguzki, a "herb gatherer" and healer, who could "see deeply into the secrets of nature." Rudolf Steiner will meet and study with this "emissary of the Master" throughout his time in Vienna.

1881: January: "... I didn't sleep a wink. I was busy with philosophical problems until about 12:30 a.m. Then, finally, I threw myself down on my couch. All my striving during the previous year had been to research whether the following statement by Schelling was true or not: *Within everyone dwells a secret, marvelous capacity to draw back from the stream of time—out of the self clothed in all that comes to us from outside—into our innermost being and there, in the immutable form of the Eternal, to look into ourselves.* I believe, and I am still quite certain of it, that I discovered this capacity in myself; I had long had an inkling of it. Now the whole of idealist philosophy stood before me in modified form. What's a sleepless night compared to that!"

Rudolf Steiner begins communicating with leading thinkers of the day, who send him books in return, which he reads eagerly.

July: "I am not one of those who dives into the day like an animal in human form. I pursue a quite specific goal, an idealistic aim—knowledge of the truth! This cannot be done offhandedly. It requires the greatest striving in the world, free of all egotism, and equally of all resignation."

August: Steiner puts down on paper for the first time thoughts for a "Philosophy of Freedom." "The striving for the absolute: this human yearning is freedom." He also seeks to outline a "peasant philosophy," describing what the worldview of a "peasant"—one who lives close to the earth and the old ways—really is.

1881-1882: Felix Koguzki, the herb gatherer, reveals himself to be the envoy of another, higher initiatory personality, who instructs Rudolf Steiner to penetrate Fichte's philosophy and to master modern scientific thinking as a preparation for right entry into the spirit. This "Master" also teaches him the double (evolutionary and involutionary) nature of time.

1882: Through the offices of Karl Julius Schröer, Rudolf Steiner is asked by Joseph Kurschner to edit Goethe's scientific works for the *Deutschen National-Literatur* edition. He writes "A Possible Critique of Atomistic Concepts" and sends it to Friedrich Theodore Vischer.

1883: Rudolf Steiner completes his college studies and begins work on the Goethe project.

1884: First volume of Goethe's *Scientific Writings* (CW 1) appears (March). He lectures on Goethe and Lessing, and Goethe's approach to science. In July, he enters the household of Ladislaus and Pauline Specht as tutor to the four Specht boys. He will live there until 1890. At this time, he meets Josef Breuer (1842-1925), the coauthor with Sigmund Freud of *Studies in Hysteria*, who is the Specht family doctor.

1885: While continuing to edit Goethe's writings, Rudolf Steiner reads deeply in contemporary philosophy (Edouard von Hartmann, Johannes Volkelt, and Richard Wahle, among others).

1886: May: Rudolf Steiner sends Kurschner the manuscript of *Outlines of Goethe's Theory of Knowledge* (CW 2), which appears in October, and which he sends out widely. He also meets the poet Marie Eugenie Delle Grazie and writes "Nature and Our Ideals" for her. He attends her salon, where he meets many priests, theologians, and philosophers, who will become his friends. Meanwhile, the director of the Goethe Archive in Weimar requests his collaboration with the *Sophien* edition of Goethe's works, particularly the writings on color.

1887: At the beginning of the year, Rudolf Steiner is very sick. As the year progresses and his health improves, he becomes increasingly "a man of letters," lecturing, writing essays, and taking part in Austrian cultural life. In August-September, the second volume of Goethe's *Scientific Writings* appears.

1888: January-July: Rudolf Steiner assumes editorship of the "German Weekly" (*Deutsche Wochenschrift*). He begins lecturing more intensively, giving, for example, a lecture titled "Goethe as Father of a New Aesthetics." He meets and becomes soul friends with Friedrich Eckstein (1861-1939), a vegetarian, philosopher of symbolism, alchemist, and musician, who will introduce him to various spiritual currents (including Theosophy) and with whom he will meditate and interpret esoteric and alchemical texts.

1889: Rudolf Steiner first reads Nietzsche (*Beyond Good and Evil*). He encounters Theosophy again and learns of Madame Blavatsky in the Theosophical circle around Marie Lang (1858-1934). Here he also meets well-known figures of Austrian life, as well as esoteric figures like the occultist Franz Hartman and Karl Leinigen-Billigen (translator of C.G. Harrison's *The Transcendental Universe.*) During this period, Steiner first reads A.P. Sinnett's *Esoteric Buddhism* and Mabel Collins's *Light on the Path.* He also begins traveling, visiting Budapest, Weimar, and Berlin (where he meets philosopher Edouard von Hartmann).

1890: Rudolf Steiner finishes volume 3 of Goethe's scientific writings. He begins his doctoral dissertation, which will become *Truth and Science* (CW 3). He also meets the poet and feminist Rosa Mayreder (1858-1938), with whom he can exchange his most intimate thoughts. In September, Rudolf Steiner moves to Weimar to work in the Goethe-Schiller Archive.

1891: Volume 3 of the Kurschner edition of Goethe appears. Meanwhile, Rudolf Steiner edits Goethe's studies in mineralogy and scientific writings for the *Sophien* edition. He meets Ludwig Laistner of the Cotta Publishing Company, who asks for a book on the basic question of metaphysics. From this will result, ultimately, *The Philosophy of Freedom* (CW 4), which will be published not by Cotta but by Emil Felber. In October, Rudolf Steiner takes the oral exam for a doctorate in philosophy, mathematics, and mechanics at Rostock University, receiving his doctorate on the twenty-sixth. In November, he gives his first lecture on Goethe's "Fairy Tale" in Vienna.

1892: Rudolf Steiner continues work at the Goethe-Schiller Archive and on his *Philosophy of Freedom. Truth and Science*, his doctoral dissertation, is published. Steiner undertakes to write introductions to books on Schopenhauer and Jean Paul for Cotta. At year's end, he finds lodging with Anna Eunike, née Schulz (1853-1911), a widow with four daughters and a son. He also develops a friendship with Otto Erich Hartleben (1864-1905) with whom he shares literary interests.

1893: Rudolf Steiner begins his habit of producing many reviews and articles. In March, he gives a lecture titled "Hypnotism, with Reference to Spiritism." In September, volume 4 of the Kurschner edition is completed. In November, *The Philosophy of Freedom* appears. This year, too, he meets John Henry Mackay (1864-1933), the anarchist, scholar, and biographer of Max Stirner.

1894: Rudolf Steiner meets Elisabeth Förster Nietzsche, the philosopher's sister, and begins to read Nietzsche in earnest, beginning with the as yet unpublished *Antichrist*. He also meets Ernst Haeckel (1834-1919). In the fall, he begins to write *Nietzsche, A Fighter against His Time* (CW 5).

1895: May, *Nietzsche, A Fighter against His Time* appears.

1896: January 22: Rudolf Steiner sees Friedrich Nietzsche for the first and only time. Moves between the Nietzsche and the Goethe-Schiller Archives, where he completes his work before year's end. He falls out with Elisabeth Förster Nietzsche, thus ending his association with the Nietzsche Archive.

1897: Rudolf Steiner finishes the manuscript of *Goethe's Worldview* (CW 6). He moves to Berlin with Anna Eunike and begins editorship of the *Magazin fur Literatur*. From now on, Steiner will write countless reviews, literary and philosophical articles, and so on. He begins lecturing at the "Free Literary Society." In September, he attends the Zionist Congress in Basel. He sides with Dreyfus in the Dreyfus affair.

1898: Rudolf Steiner is very active as an editor in the political, artistic, and theatrical life of Berlin. He becomes friendly with John Henry Mackay and poet Ludwig Jacobowski (1868-1900). He joins Jacobowski's circle of writers, artists, and scientists—"The Coming Ones" (*Die Kommenden*)—and contributes lectures to the group until 1903. He also lectures at the "League for College Pedagogy." He writes an article for Goethe's sesquicentennial, "Goethe's Secret Revelation," on the "Fairy Tale of the Green Snake and the Beautiful Lily."

1898-99: "This was a trying time for my soul as I looked at Christianity.... I was able to progress only by contemplating, by means of spiritual perception, the evolution of Christianity .... Conscious knowledge of real Christianity began to dawn in me around the turn of the century. This seed continued to develop. My soul trial occurred shortly before the beginning of the twentieth century. It was decisive for my soul's development that I stood spiritually before the Mystery of Golgotha in a deep and solemn celebration of knowledge "

1899: Rudolf Steiner begins teaching and giving lectures and lecture cycles at the Workers' College, founded by Wilhelm Liebknecht (1826-1900). He will continue to do so until 1904. Writes: *Literature and Spiritual Life in the Nineteenth Century; Individualism in Philosophy; Haeckel and His Opponents; Poetry in the Present;* and begins what will become (fifteen years later) *The Riddles of Philosophy* (CW 18). He also meets many artists and writers, including Käthe Kollwitz, Stefan Zweig, and Rainer Maria Rilke. On October 31, he marries Anna Eunike.

1900: "I thought that the turn of the century must bring humanity a new light. It seemed to me that the separation of human thinking and willing from the spirit had peaked. A turn or reversal of direction in human evolution seemed to me a necessity." Rudolf Steiner finishes *World and Life Views in the Nineteenth Century* (the second part of what will become *The Riddles of Philosophy*) and dedicates it to Ernst Haeckel. It is published in March. He continues lecturing at *Die Kommenden*, whose leadership he assumes after the death of Jacobowski. Also, he gives the Gutenberg Jubilee lecture before 7,000 typesetters and printers. In September, Rudolf Steiner is invited by Count and Countess Brockdorff to lecture in the Theosophical Library. His first lecture is on Nietzsche. His second lecture is titled "Goethe's Secret Revelation." October 6, he begins a lecture cycle on the mystics that will become *Mystics after Modernism* (CW 7). November-December: "Marie von Sivers appears in the audience...." Also in November, Steiner gives his first lecture at the Giordano Bruno Bund (where he will continue to lecture until May, 1905). He speaks on Bruno and modern Rome, focusing on the importance of the philosophy of Thomas Aquinas as monism.

1901: In continual financial straits, Rudolf Steiner's early friends Moritz Zitter and Rosa Mayreder help support him. In October, he begins the lecture cycle *Christianity as Mystical Fact* (CW 8) at the Theosophical Library. In November, he gives his first "Theosophical lecture" on Goethe's "Fairy Tale" in Hamburg at the invitation of Wilhelm Hubbe-Schleiden. He also attends a gathering to celebrate the founding of the Theosophical Society at Count and Countess Brockdorff's. He gives a lecture cycle, "From Buddha to Christ," for the circle of the *Kommenden*. November 17, Marie von Sivers asks Rudolf Steiner if Theosophy needs a Western-Christian spiritual movement (to complement Theosophy's Eastern emphasis). "The question was posed. Now, following spiritual laws, I could begin to give an answer...." In December, Rudolf Steiner writes his first article for a Theosophical publication. At year's end, the Brockdorffs and possibly Wilhelm Hubbe-Schleiden ask Rudolf Steiner to join the Theosophical Society and undertake the leadership of the German section. Rudolf Steiner agrees, on the condition that Marie von Sivers (then in Italy) work with him.

1902: Beginning in January, Rudolf Steiner attends the opening of the Workers' School in Spandau with Rosa Luxemberg (1870-1919). January 17, Rudolf Steiner joins the Theosophical Society. In April, he is asked to become general secretary of the German Section of the Theosophical Society, and works on preparations for its founding. In July, he visits London for a Theosophical congress. He meets Bertram Keightly, G.R.S. Mead, A.P. Sinnett, and Annie Besant, among others. In September, *Christianity as Mystical Fact* appears. In October, Rudolf

Steiner gives his first public lecture on Theosophy ("Monism and Theosophy") to about three hundred people at the Giordano Bruno Bund. On October 19-21, the German Section of the Theosophical Society has its first meeting; Rudolf Steiner is the general secretary, and Annie Besant attends. Steiner lectures on practical karma studies. On October 23, Annie Besant inducts Rudolf Steiner into the Esoteric School of the Theosophical Society. On October 25, Steiner begins a weekly series of lectures: "The Field of Theosophy." During this year, Rudolf Steiner also meets Ita Wegman (1876-1943), who will become his close collaborator in his final years.

1903: Rudolf Steiner holds about 300 lectures and seminars. In May, the first issue of the periodical *Luzifer* appears. In June, Rudolf Steiner visits London for the first meeting of the Federation of the European Sections of the Theosophical Society, where he meets Colonel Olcott. He begins to write *Theosophy* (CW 9).

1904: Rudolf Steiner continues lecturing at the Workers' College and elsewhere (about 90 lectures), while lecturing intensively all over Germany among Theosophists (about 140 lectures). In February, he meets Carl Unger (1878-1929), who will become a member of the board of the Anthroposophical Society (1913). In March, he meets Michael Bauer (1871-1929), a Christian mystic, who will also be on the board. In May, *Theosophy* appears, with the dedication: "To the spirit of Giordano Bruno." Rudolf Steiner and Marie von Sivers visit London for meetings with Annie Besant. June: Rudolf Steiner and Marie von Sivers attend the meeting of the Federation of European Sections of the Theosophical Society in Amsterdam. In July, Steiner begins the articles in *Luzifer-Gnosis* that will become *How to Know Higher Worlds* (CW 10) and *Cosmic Memory* (CW 11). In September, Annie Besant visits Germany. In December, Steiner lectures on Freemasonry. He mentions the High Grade Masonry derived from John Yarker and represented by Theodore Reuss and Karl Kellner as a blank slate "into which a good image could be placed."

1905: This year, Steiner ends his non-Theosophical lecturing activity. Supported by Marie von Sivers, his Theosophical lecturing—both in public and in the Theosophical Society—increases significantly: "The German Theosophical Movement is of exceptional importance." Steiner recommends reading, among others, Fichte, Jacob Boehme, and Angelus Silesius. He begins to introduce Christian themes into Theosophy. He also begins to work with doctors (Felix Peipers and Ludwig Noll). In July, he is in London for the Federation of European Sections, where he attends a lecture by Annie Besant: "I have seldom seen Mrs. Besant speak in so inward and heartfelt a manner...." "Through Mrs. Besant I have found the way to H.P. Blavatsky." September to October, he gives a course of thirty-one lectures for a small group of esoteric students. In October, the annual meeting of the German Section of the Theosophical Society, which still remains very small, takes place. Rudolf Steiner reports membership has risen from 121 to 377 members. In November, seeking to establish esoteric "continuity," Rudolf Steiner and Marie von Sivers participate in a "Memphis-Misraim" Masonic ceremony. They pay forty-five marks for membership. "Yesterday, you saw how little remains of former esoteric institutions." "We are dealing only with a 'framework'... for the present, nothing lies behind it. The occult powers have completely withdrawn."

1906: Expansion of Theosophical work. Rudolf Steiner gives about 245 lectures, only 44 of which take place in Berlin. Cycles are given in Paris, Leipzig, Stuttgart, and Munich. Esoteric work also intensifies. Rudolf Steiner begins writing *An Outline of Esoteric Science* (CW 13). In January, Rudolf Steiner receives permission (a patent) from the Great Orient of the Scottish A & A Thirty-Three Degree Rite of the Order of the Ancient Freemasons of the Memphis-Misraim Rite to direct a chapter under the name "Mystica Aeterna." This will become the "Cognitive-Ritual Section" (also called "Misraim Service") of the Esoteric School. (See: *Freemasonry and Ritual Work: The Misraim Service* (CW 265). During this time, Steiner also meets Albert Schweitzer. In May, he is in Paris, where he visits Edouard Schuré. Many Russians attend his lectures (including Konstantin Balmont, Dimitri Mereszkovski, Zinaida Hippius, and Maximilian Woloshin). He attends the General Meeting of the European Federation of the Theosophical Society, at which Col. Olcott is present for the last time. He spends the year's end in Venice and Rome, where he writes and works on his translation of H.P. Blavatsky's *Key to Theosophy*.

1907: Further expansion of the German Theosophical Movement according to the Rosicrucian directive to "introduce spirit into the world"—in education, in social questions, in art, and in science. In February, Col. Olcott dies in Adyar. Before he dies, Olcott indicates that "the Masters" wish Annie Besant to succeed him: much politicking ensues. Rudolf Steiner supports Besant's candidacy. April-May: preparations for the Congress of the Federation of European Sections of the Theosophical Society—the great, watershed Whitsun "Munich Congress," attended by Annie Besant and others. Steiner decides to separate Eastern and Western (Christian-Rosicrucian) esoteric schools. He takes his esoteric school out of the Theosophical Society (Besant and Rudolf Steiner are "in harmony" on this). Steiner makes his first lecture tours to Austria and Hungary. That summer, he is in Italy. In September, he visits Edouard Schuré, who will write the introduction to the French edition of *Christianity as Mystical Fact* in Barr, Alsace. Rudolf Steiner writes the autobiographical statement known as the "Barr Document." In *Luzifer–Gnosis*, "The Education of the Child" appears.

1908: The movement grows (membership: 1,150). Lecturing expands. Steiner makes his first extended lecture tour to Holland and Scandinavia, as well as visits to Naples and Sicily. Themes: St. John's Gospel, the Apocalypse, Egypt, science, philosophy, and logic. *Luzifer-Gnosis* ceases publication. In Berlin, Marie von Sivers (with Johanna Mücke (1864-1949) forms the *Philosophisch-Theosophisch* (after 1915 *Philosophisch-Anthroposophisch*) *Verlag* to publish Steiner's work. Steiner gives lecture cycles titled *The Gospel of St. John* (CW 103) and *The Apocalypse* (104).

1909: *An Outline of Esoteric Science* appears. Lecturing and travel continues. Rudolf Steiner's spiritual research expands to include the polarity of Lucifer and Ahriman; the work of great individualities in history; the Maitreya Buddha and the Bodhisattvas; spiritual economy (CW 109); the work of the spiritual hierarchies in heaven and on earth (CW 110). He also deepens and intensifies his research into the Gospels, giving lectures on the Gospel of St. Luke (CW 114) with the first mention of two Jesus children. Meets and becomes friends with Christian Morgenstern (1871-1914). In April, he lays the foundation stone for the Malsch model—the building that will lead to the first Goetheanum. In May, the International Congress of the Federation of European Sections of the Theosophical Society takes place in Budapest. Rudolf Steiner receives the Subba Row medal for *How to Know Higher Worlds*. During this time, Charles W. Leadbeater discovers Jiddu Krishnamurti (1895-1986) and proclaims him the future "world teacher," the bearer of the Maitreya Buddha and the "reappearing Christ." In October, Steiner delivers seminal lectures on "anthroposophy," which he will try, unsuccessfully, to rework over the next years into the unfinished work, *Anthroposophy (A Fragment)* (CW 45).

1910: New themes: *The Reappearance of Christ in the Etheric* (CW 118); *The Fifth Gospel; The Mission of Folk Souls* (CW 121); *Occult History* (CW 126); the evolving development of etheric cognitive capacities. Rudolf Steiner continues his Gospel research with *The Gospel of St. Matthew* (CW 123). In January, his father dies. In April, he takes a month-long trip to Italy, including Rome, Monte Cassino, and Sicily. He also visits Scandinavia again. July-August, he writes the first mystery drama, *The Portal of Initiation* (CW 14). In November, he gives "psychosophy" lectures. In December, he submits "On the Psychological Foundations and Epistemological Framework of Theosophy" to the International Philosophical Congress in Bologna.

1911: The crisis in the Theosophical Society deepens. In January, "The Order of the Rising Sun," which will soon become "The Order of the Star in the East," is founded for the coming world teacher, Krishnamurti. At the same time, Marie von Sivers, Rudolf Steiner's coworker, falls ill. Fewer lectures are given, but important new ground is broken. In Prague, in March, Steiner meets Franz Kafka (1883-1924) and Hugo Bergmann (1883-1975). In April, he delivers his paper to the Philosophical Congress. He writes the second mystery drama, *The Soul's Probation* (CW 14). Also, while Marie von Sivers is convalescing, Rudolf Steiner begins work on *Calendar 1912/1913*, which will contain the "Calendar of the Soul" meditations. On March 19, Anna (Eunike) Steiner dies. In September, Rudolf Steiner visits Einsiedeln, birthplace of Paracelsus. In December, Friedrich Rittelmeyer, future founder of the Christian Community, meets Rudolf Steiner. The *Johannes-Bauverein*, the "building committee," which would lead to the first Goetheanum (first planned for Munich), is also founded, and a preliminary committee for the founding of an independent association is created that, in the following year, will become the Anthroposophical Society. Important lecture cycles include *Occult Physiology* (CW 128); *Wonders of the World* (CW 129); *From Jesus to Christ* (CW 131). Other themes: esoteric Christianity; Christian Rosenkreutz; the spiritual guidance of humanity; the sense world and the world of the spirit.

1912: Despite the ongoing, now increasing crisis in the Theosophical Society, much is accomplished: *Calendar 1912/1913* is published; eurythmy is created; both the third mystery drama, *The Guardian of the Threshold* (CW 14) and *A Way of Self-Knowledge* (CW 16) are written. New (or renewed) themes included life between death and rebirth and karma and reincarnation. Other lecture cycles: *Spiritual Beings in the Heavenly Bodies and in the Kingdoms of Nature* (CW 136); *The Human Being in the Light of Occultism, Theosophy, and Philosophy* (CW 137); *The Gospel of St. Mark* (CW 139); and *The Bhagavad Gita and the Epistles of Paul* (CW 142). On May 8, Rudolf Steiner celebrates White Lotus Day, H.P. Blavatsky's death day, which he had faithfully observed for the past decade, for the last time. In August, Rudolf Steiner suggests the "independent association" be called the "Anthroposophical Society." In September, the first eurythmy course takes place. In October, Rudolf Steiner declines recognition of a Theosophical Society lodge dedicated to the Star of the East and decides to expel all Theosophical Society members belonging to the order. Also, with Marie von Sivers, he first visits Dornach, near Basel, Switzerland, and they stand on the hill where the Goetheanum will be built. In November, a Theosophical Society lodge is opened by direct mandate from Adyar (Annie Besant). In December, a meeting of the German section occurs at which it is decided that belonging to the Order of the Star of the East is incompatible with membership in the Theosophical Society. December 28: informal founding of the Anthroposophical Society in Berlin.

1913: Expulsion of the German section from the Theosophical Society. February 2-3: Foundation meeting of the Anthroposophical Society. Board members include: Marie von Sivers, Michael Bauer, and Carl Unger. September 20: Laying of the foundation stone for the *Johannes Bau* (Goetheanum) in Dornach. Building begins immediately. The third mystery drama, *The Soul's Awakening* (CW 14), is completed. Also: *The Threshold of the Spiritual World* (CW 147). Lecture cycles include: *The Bhagavad Gita and the Epistles of Paul* and *The*

Esoteric Meaning of the Bhagavad Gita (CW 146), which the Russian philosopher Nikolai Berdyaev attends; *The Mysteries of the East and of Christianity* (CW 144); *The Effects of Esoteric Development* (CW 145); and *The Fifth Gospel* (CW 148). In May, Rudolf Steiner is in London and Paris, where anthroposophical work continues.

1914: Building continues on the *Johannes Bau* (Goetheanum) in Dornach, with artists and coworkers from seventeen nations. The general assembly of the Anthroposophical Society takes place. In May, Rudolf Steiner visits Paris, as well as Chartres Cathedral. June 28: assassination in Sarajevo ("Now the catastrophe has happened!"). August 1: War is declared. Rudolf Steiner returns to Germany from Dornach—he will travel back and forth. He writes the last chapter of *The Riddles of Philosophy*. Lecture cycles include: *Human and Cosmic Thought* (CW 151); *Inner Being of Humanity between Death and a New Birth* (CW 153); *Occult Reading and Occult Hearing* (CW 156). December 24: marriage of Rudolf Steiner and Marie von Sivers.

1915: Building continues. Life after death becomes a major theme, also art. Writes: *Thoughts during a Time of War* (CW 24). Lectures include: *The Secret of Death* (CW 159); *The Uniting of Humanity through the Christ Impulse* (CW 165).

1916: Rudolf Steiner begins work with Edith Maryon (1872-1924) on the sculpture "The Representative of Humanity" ("The Group"—Christ, Lucifer, and Ahriman). He also works with the alchemist Alexander von Bernus on the quarterly *Das Reich*. He writes *The Riddle of Humanity* (CW 20). Lectures include: *Necessity and Freedom in World History and Human Action* (CW 166); *Past and Present in the Human Spirit* (CW 167); *The Karma of Vocation* (CW 172); *The Karma of Untruthfulness* (CW 173).

1917: Russian Revolution. The U.S. enters the war. Building continues. Rudolf Steiner delineates the idea of the "threefold nature of the human being" (in a public lecture March 15) and the "threefold nature of the social organism" (hammered out in May-June with the help of Otto von Lerchenfeld and Ludwig Polzer-Hoditz in the form of two documents titled *Memoranda*, which were distributed in high places). August-September: Rudolf Steiner writes *The Riddles of the Soul* (CW 20). Also: commentary on "The Chemical Wedding of Christian Rosenkreutz" for Alexander Bernus (*Das Reich*). Lectures include: *The Karma of Materialism* (CW 176); *The Spiritual Background of the Outer World: The Fall of the Spirits of Darkness* (CW 177).

1918: March 18: peace treaty of Brest-Litovsk—"Now everything will truly enter chaos! What is needed is cultural renewal." June: Rudolf Steiner visits Karlstein (Grail) Castle outside Prague. Lecture cycle: *From Symptom to Reality in Modern History* (CW 185). In mid-November, Emil Molt, of the Waldorf-Astoria Cigarette Company, has the idea of founding a school for his workers' children.

1919: Focus on the threefold social organism: tireless travel, countless lectures, meetings, and publications. At the same time, a new public stage of Anthroposophy emerges as cultural renewal begins. The coming years will see initiatives in pedagogy, medicine, pharmacology, and agriculture. January 27: threefold meeting: " We must first of all, with the money we have, found free schools that can bring people what they need." February: first public eurythmy performance in Zurich. Also: "Appeal to the German People" (CW 24), circulated March 6 as a newspaper insert. In April, *Towards Social Renewal* (CW 23) appears—"perhaps the most widely read of all books on politics appearing since the war." Rudolf Steiner is asked to undertake the "direction and leadership" of the school founded by the Waldorf-Astoria Company. Rudolf Steiner begins to talk about the "renewal" of education. May 30: a building is selected and purchased for the future Waldorf School. August-September, Rudolf Steiner gives a lecture course for Waldorf teachers, *The Foundations of Human Experience (Study of Man)* (CW 293). September 7: Opening of the first Waldorf School. December (into January): first science course, the *Light Course* (CW 320).

1920: The Waldorf School flourishes. New threefold initiatives. Founding of limited companies *Der Kommende Tag* and *Futurum A.G.* to infuse spiritual values into the economic realm. Rudolf Steiner also focuses on the sciences. Lectures: *Introducing Anthroposophical Medicine* (CW 312); *The Warmth Course* (CW 321); *The Boundaries of Natural Science* (CW 322); *The Redemption of Thinking* (CW 74). February: Johannes Werner Klein—later a cofounder of the Christian Community—asks Rudolf Steiner about the possibility of a "religious renewal," a "Johannine church." In March, Rudolf Steiner gives the first course for doctors and medical students. In April, a divinity student asks Rudolf Steiner a second time about the possibility of religious renewal. September 27-October 16: anthroposophical "university course." December: lectures titled *The Search for the New Isis* (CW 202).

1921: Rudolf Steiner continues his intensive work on cultural renewal, including the uphill battle for the threefold social order. "University" arts, scientific, theological, and medical courses include: *The Astronomy Course* (CW 323); *Observation, Mathematics, and Scientific Experiment* (CW 324); the *Second Medical Course* (CW 313); *Color.* In June and September-October, Rudolf Steiner also gives the first two "priests' courses" (CW 342 and 343). The "youth movement" gains momentum. Magazines are founded: *Die Drei* (January), and—under the editorship of Albert Steffen (1884-1963)—the weekly, *Das Goetheanum* (August). In February-March, Rudolf Steiner takes his first trip outside Germany since the war (Holland). On April 7, Steiner receives a letter regarding "religious renewal," and May 22-23, he agrees to address the question in a practical way. In June, the Klinical-Therapeutic Institute opens in Arlesheim under the direction of Dr. Ita Wegman. In August, the Chemical-Pharmaceutical Laboratory opens in Arlesheim (Oskar Schmiedel and Ita Wegman are directors). The Clinical Therapeutic Institute is inaugurated in Stuttgart (Dr. Ludwig Noll is director); also the Research Laboratory in Dornach (Ehrenfried Pfeiffer and Gunther Wachsmuth are directors). In November-December, Rudolf Steiner visits Norway.

1922: The first half of the year involves very active public lecturing (thousands attend); in the second half, Rudolf Steiner begins to withdraw and turn toward the Society—"The Society is asleep." It is "too weak" to do what is asked of it. The businesses—*Der Kommende Tag* and *Futura A.G.*—fail. In January, with the help of an agent, Steiner undertakes a twelve-city German lecture tour, accompanied by eurythmy performances. In two weeks he speaks to more than 2,000 people. In April, he gives a "university course" in The Hague. He also visits England. In June, he is in Vienna for the East-West Congress. In August-September, he is back in England for the Oxford Conference on Education. Returning to Dornach, he gives the lectures *Philosophy, Cosmology, and Religion* (CW 215), and gives the third priests' course (CW 344). On September 16, The Christian Community is founded. In October-November, Steiner is in Holland and England. He also speaks to the youth: *The Youth Course* (CW 217). In December, Steiner gives lectures titled *The Origins of Natural Science* (CW 326), and *Humanity and the World of Stars: The Spiritual Communion of Humanity* (CW 219). December 31: Fire at the Goetheanum, which is destroyed.

1923: Despite the fire, Rudolf Steiner continues his work unabated. A very hard year. Internal dispersion, dissension, and apathy abound. There is conflict—between old and new visions—within the society. A wake-up call is needed, and Rudolf Steiner responds with renewed lecturing vitality. His focus: the spiritual context of human life; initiation science; the course of the year; and community building. As a foundation for an artistic school, he creates a series of pastel sketches. Lecture cycles: *The Anthroposophical Movement; Initiation Science* (CW 227) (in England at the Penmaenmawr Summer School); *The Four Seasons and the Archangels* (CW 229); *Harmony of the Creative Word* (CW 230); *The Supersensible Human* (CW 231), given in Holland for the founding of the Dutch society. On November 10, in response to the failed Hitler-Ludendorf putsch in Munich, Steiner closes his Berlin residence and moves the *Philosophisch-Anthroposophisch Verlag* (Press) to Dornach. On December 9, Steiner begins the serialization of his *Autobiography: The Course of My Life* (CW 28) in *Das Goetheanum*. It will continue to appear weekly, without a break, until his death. Late December-early January: Rudolf Steiner refounds the Anthroposophical Society (about 12,000 members internationally) and takes over its leadership. The new board members are: Marie Steiner, Ita Wegman, Albert Steffen, Elizabeth Vreede, and Guenther Wachsmuth. (See *The Christmas*

Meeting for the Founding of the General Anthroposophical Society (CW 260). Accompanying lectures: *Mystery Knowledge and Mystery Centers* (CW 232); *World History in the Light of Anthroposophy* (CW 233). December 25: the Foundation Stone is laid (in the hearts of members) in the form of the "Foundation Stone Meditation."

1924: January 1: having founded the Anthroposophical Society and taken over its leadership, Rudolf Steiner has the task of "reforming" it. The process begins with a weekly newssheet ("What's Happening in the Anthroposophical Society") in which Rudolf Steiner's "Letters to Members" and "Anthroposophical Leading Thoughts" appear (CW 26). The next step is the creation of a new esoteric class, the "first class" of the "University of Spiritual Science" (which was to have been followed, had Rudolf Steiner lived longer, by two more advanced classes). Then comes a new language for Anthroposophy—practical, phenomenological, and direct; and Rudolf Steiner creates the model for the second Goetheanum. He begins the series of extensive "karma" lectures (CW 235-40); and finally, responding to needs, he creates two new initiatives: biodynamic agriculture and curative education. After the middle of the year, rumors begin to circulate regarding Steiner's health. Lectures: January-February, *Anthroposophy* (CW 234); February: *Tone Eurythmy* (CW 278); June: *The Agriculture Course* (CW 327); June-July: Speech [?] Eurythmy (CW 279); *Curative Education* (CW 317); August: (England, "Second International Summer School"), *Initiation Consciousness: True and False Paths in Spiritual Investigation* (CW 243); September: *Pastoral Medicine* (CW 318). On September 26, for the first time, Rudolf Steiner cancels a lecture. On September 28, he gives his last lecture. On September 29, he withdraws to his studio in the carpenter's shop; now he is definitively ill. Cared for by Ita Wegman, he continues working, however, and writing the weekly installments of his *Autobiography* and *Letters to the Members/Leading Thoughts* (CW 26).

1925: Rudolf Steiner, while continuing to work, continues to weaken. He finishes *Extending Practical Medicine* (CW 27) with Ita Wegman.

On March 30, around ten in the morning, Rudolf Steiner dies.

INDEX